Studying Insects

A PRACTICAL GUIDE

Studying Insects

A PRACTICAL GUIDE

R. L. E. FORD

WITH 47 LINE DRAWINGS
AND 16 PAGES OF PLATES IN
COLOUR AND BLACK-AND-WHITE

FREDERICK WARNE
LONDON   NEW YORK

Published by
FREDERICK WARNE & CO LTD: *London*
FREDERICK WARNE & CO INC: *New York*

© *Frederick Warne & Co Ltd 1973*

PUBLISHER'S NOTE
This book is a fully revised edition of the 1963 Warne publication *Practical Entomology*, by the same author.

LINE DRAWINGS BY GORDON RILEY
COLOUR PHOTOGRAPHS BY ROBIN FLETCHER

*LIBRARY OF CONGRESS CATALOG
CARD NO. 73-75027*

ISBN 0 7232 1705 X

*Text set in 12 pt. Photon Times, printed by photolithography,
and bound in Great Britain at The Pitman Press, Bath*
440.373

Contents

List of Plates	viii
Preface	xi
Conservation: AN ENTOMOLOGIST'S NOTES	1
Insect Classification	11
Insect Structure: DEVELOPMENT AND FUNCTIONS	19

The Perfect Insect — 24

CATCHING — 24
Butterflies Nets old and new Use of bait
Moths Mercury vapour traps Lamps Sugaring
Assembling moths
Adult microlepidoptera Bee smokers Beating thatch Jarring trees
Other insects Sweeping Collecting from flower heads Traps

KILLING — 42
Charging a killing bottle Types of chemical Use of hypodermic syringe Reversing wings

RELAXING — 45
Relaxing tins Papering foreign specimens Relaxing microlepidoptera

SETTING — 47
Boards Pins Pin chart Storage and setting houses

MOUNTING — 55
Beetles on cards Hymenoptera Pinning stages

Breeding — 60

THE EGG STAGE — 60
Butterflies Laying tubs Artificial feeding Clouded yellow method
Moths Hawk moths Materials for oviposition

CONTENTS

COLLECTING LARVAE 63
Butterflies Beating Searching Night collecting 'Blues'
Moths Searching Sweeping Microlepidoptera

THE CATERPILLAR STAGE 68
Cages
Sleeving larvae
The care of young caterpillars
Rearing silk-worms

THE CHRYSALIS STAGE 75
Pupation Keeping down mould
Storing pupae
Emergence
Sexing pupae
Pupa digging
Forcing pupae

FURTHER BREEDING METHODS 79
Microlepidoptera Searching Breeding in flower-pots Humidity control Emergence Over-wintering Keeping plant material
Plant tubs

Preserving Larvae 86
Larvae 'blowing' Large and hairy larvae Microlepidoptera larvae
Mounting
Colouring
The 'freeze-drying' technique
Storing larvae in fluid

Labelling and Care of Collections 93
Labels
Storage boxes
Cabinets
Converting or reconditioning cabinets or boxes Corking
Papering and repapering
Grease and degreasing Repinning
Repairing damaged specimens
Insect deterrents
Mould Easing drawers

Ants 109
MAKING A FORMICARIUM 109
Collecting stocks
Feeding

Wasps in Captivity 114
Collecting and establishing nests Tracking nests

CONTENTS

Humble-bees	117
Caring for and protecting wild nests Nesting sites for other wild bees	
A Sub-terrarium	119
Illustrating Insects	121
Attracting Butterflies and Moths to your Garden	124
Insect Cultures	128
Identification of Insects	133
Appendix I: A Code for Insect Collecting	135
Appendix II: Times of Appearance of British Butterflies	139
Appendix III: Food Plants of British Butterflies	141
Appendix IV: Books, Magazines, Societies and Supplies	143
Indexes	146

List of Plates

Plate 1	Examining the contents of a mercury vapour moth-trap Planting out young Cicada grubs
Plate 2	Using a kite net as a beating tray under thatch Smoking out adult microlepidoptera
Plate 3	Early collectors with a 'bat-fouler' net in foreground The end of a stroke with a kite net
Plate 4	The only English Cicada, *Cicadetta montana*, from the New Forest Grub of the New Forest Cicada
Plate 5	Burying Beetle, *Necrophorus vespillo*, on rabbit fur Caddis-fly (adult) at rest on a rush
Plate 6	Sugaring old tree-stumps Wooden travelling setting-board case
Plate 7	Egg-laying tub ready for butterflies An M.V. moth-trap assembled
Plate 8	Dor Beetle with mites clinging to its underside Rose Chafer, *Cetonia aurata*, on an elder flower
Plate 9	Wood Wasp, female, *Sirex gigas*, ovipositing Grub of the Cockchafer Beetle
Plate 10	Placing sleeves for larvae on bushes Beating large trees with a sheet
Plate 11	A folding beating tray (Bignall pattern) Digging pupae at the base of a tree
Plate 12	Common Blue, female, *Polyommatus icarus* Cinnabar Moth, *Callimorpha jacobaeae*
Plate 13	Large Marsh Grasshopper, *Stethophyma grossum* Bush Cricket, *Tettigonia viridissima*

LIST OF PLATES

Plate 14   A battery of cylinder cages
Using Wild microscope when drawing specimens

Plate 15   Early form of microprojector
Photographing specimens through the microscope

Plate 16   Bush Cricket, *Leptophytes punctatissima*
Wood Cricket, *Nemobius sylvestris*
Bush Cricket, *Platycleis denticulata*
Tree Wasp, *Vespula sylvestris*, nest

Preface

Few hobbies can be so pleasant and instructive as that of entomology, the science of the study of insects. It takes one into the more remote and beautiful parts of the country, often in the company of others with similar interests, and one invariably learns more than one expects. The student develops a growing interest in the activities of insects and their biological cycle, and their relationship with other forms of life.

Even the serious scientist, anxious to collect more species and hoping to find caterpillars and eggs, will refer to books to see what a certain butterfly feeds on. This means that soon he will be taking an interest in plants and learning their names. To find plants he may look for certain types of habitat and soil, so that a little elementary geology will not come amiss.

Another advantage of this hobby is one denied to many sportsmen: one can study indoors when it rains. There will be names to look up, facts to check, specimens to arrange and label and, I hope, notes to write. If you approach a hobby in this manner you will be not merely another collector with a row of specimens but a contributor to knowledge. If one thinks of the tremendous effect of insect activities on those of man it is clear that a pleasant hobby may easily lead to a more serious and valuable study.

The study of insects has reached a very advanced stage in the British Isles, but there are still enormous gaps in our knowledge. We now know how many species there are in most of the orders of insects, and their individual names, although in an order like that of the Hymenoptera, which includes all the Braconidae and parasitic species, there must still be a great many yet to be discovered.

In an order such as the Lepidoptera we even know virtually all the food plants and breeding habits of the group, although there are still gaps in our knowledge of the smallest species.

Among the Diptera, or two-winged flies, however, there are still

PREFACE

some quite large flies of which we know the names, but what they feed on and how they go about their affairs is still a mystery. This lack of knowledge is probably greatest in connection with the Hymenoptera. In the past, collectors would hope to breed out an attractive moth and instead get a nasty parasitic fly; in their annoyance, and possibly with the thought of saving other moths, they would stamp on the offender. If they had saved the parasitic fly and labelled it with the date, locality and, most important of all, the name of the host, then we should have by now a wonderful collection for study.

At the present time, those who become interested in insects are always inclined towards groups which are already well known simply because there is more literature about them and they can look up facts about them in a book. What we need is more people to have the courage to launch out into the lesser known groups. The scope is there and work of this sort will provide great interest and the satisfaction of adding new knowledge in this fascinating field.

AUTHOR'S NOTE

Measurements in this book are given in Imperial measurements with approximate equivalents in metric figures.

Conservation:

AN ENTOMOLOGIST'S NOTES

In recent years pressures on various areas of our countryside, in many cases of special interest to the naturalist, have become so increased that efforts to conserve what remains of them have become an obvious need. It is now hoped that a large number of sites will be preserved. Of course, not all these sites are connected with entomology. Some are scheduled purely for their natural beauty and others as sites of scientific interest, for instance, in the fields of archeology and geology, as well as botany and entomology, but obviously any areas left in their natural state are of interest to the entomologist, so diversified are the requirements of insects.

It is not sufficient, however, to reserve an area for its entomological properties and leave it at that. Lord Rothschild was the first to recognize this when he 'farmed' the Large Copper in the Wood Walton Fen. This was not the original English Large Copper which was exterminated by fen drainage and clearance. The species introduced came from Holland but closely resembled the English form. The 'farming', carried out by a resident keeper, consisted of growing and planting-out plants of the water dock on which this butterfly feeds, clearing reeds and any other obstructive growths around existing plants, collecting almost fully grown larvae and allowing them to reach maturity in captivity, and often allowing bred butterflies to mate in captivity so that fertile females could be released in desirable areas.

On the death of Lord Rothschild, when the fens were given to the nation, this work was continued by a committee, and now more recently by The Nature Conservancy who actively look into the special requirements of insects in areas under their care.

The Royal Entomological Society of London recognized that the need for similar work was essential and a committee was set up for this purpose. The work of this committee, however, was chiefly concerned with moths, and in the case of several species plant growth was deliberately cut annually to encourage the growth of special plants on which a particular moth would feed.

Often these plants would be not uncommon and occur in many places, but insects are sometimes very selective in their habits and will colonize a particular area for reasons best known to themselves. Without the aid of active entomologists these species and special places would never be discovered, reported, recorded and finally it is hoped, preserved.

This type of conservation is one of the more easily performed tasks and a very effective one in most cases. It also works well for rare plants, but it needs an interested local body to organize volunteers and funds to pay for the work done.

I first became interested in practical work of this nature when assisting and advising the late C. W. W. Hulse to preserve the Large Blue in Cornwall. This butterfly needs certain conditions for its success. Firstly, of course, the right food plant, wild thyme, on which the female lays her eggs. Possibly the first requirement should be ant-hills on which the wild thyme grows. Nearly all the suitable ant hillocks are those made by the small yellow ant, *Donisthorpea flava*. In addition to this ant and its hills, the Large Blue requires the presence of two other ants, *Myrmica scabrinodis* and *Myrmica laevinodis*. Both of these species will flourish alongside the nests of *Donisthorpea flava,* and their presence is required since they take the larvae of the Large Blue below ground for the winter months. Finally, sheep or rabbits are needed to keep the surrounding grass from becoming too long, since this will kill off the wild thyme. Too many rabbits are undesirable because they are fond of sitting on ant-hills and using them for their natural functions, which can harm the butterfly eggs and young larvae.

Certain hillsides in Devon and Cornwall are slightly rocky with poor soil and these have wild thyme over rocks as well, no tall herbage will grow, and ants will also nest under shallow rocks, which get warmed by the sun. Unfortunately Cornwall suffered at that time, and no doubt still does so, from gorse bushes. These grow rapidly, kill off all the undergrowth and exterminate the butterfly colonies. Local farmers would then burn off the gorse to improve the grazing for their sheep. This would lead to fresh young growths and the butterflies would find a new area to colonize. Unfortunately, this burning might not always be done in the winter when the ants were underground and also the fires would get far too hot, killing off everything, plants and ants.

CONSERVATION

I was first called in on this Cornish project over the matter of natural parasites but fortunately the Large Blue, almost alone amongst the British butterflies, is virtually parasite free.

Hulse secured the co-operation of a local farmer who had a large tract of land and this included a hillside with a southern aspect which was also a desirable feature. We undertook to do the actual burning off ourselves and this was done when there was as little wind as possible and with small controllable fires arranged in a wide strip. The idea was to burn strips off one year and when the new growth came up it would attract all the butterflies, and then the next winter the adjacent strip could be burnt. This worked well and was so successful that the butterflies appeared in unbelievable numbers but, unfortunately, when matters had reached a climax, Hulse died suddenly and the area became neglected again.

There is a great deal of similar, but easier, work, which not only the entomologist but the general public can undertake.

A number of British butterflies, although they are fairly widespread and not nearing extinction, require assistance as soon as possible. Amongst these are the Brimstone and the Orange-tip butterflies, both having brightly coloured males and both very attractive when flying about. The Brimstone is threatened since the larvae only eat two species of buckthorn and nothing else. One of these species, *Rhamnus cartharticus,* grows more on open ground and on limestone soils and the other *Rhamnus frangula* is more or less confined to woodlands.

The first species, *cartharticus,* suffers greatly when hedges are removed from agricultural land. At the moment the government is actually paying the farmer to do just this. The bush is not a common hedgerow species but, spread out over a wide area, it is ideal for the continuation of this butterfly since there will be small pockets which will be parasite free. There is one braconid parasite *(Apanteles gonopterygis)* which attacks this butterfly and nothing else. Fortunately it is what is termed a solitary species and not a gregarious one so that one host larva produces only one parasite and not a bunch of seventy or so. In this instance, the parasite builds up until all the Brimstone larvae on one bush will be attacked and killed. It will be perhaps nearly a mile to the next bush and possibly too far to fly, so the *Apanteles* here die out. The bush will be re-colonized next year and a fresh lot of butterflies will flourish until by chance an *Apanteles* happens to come along.

If you watch a female Brimstone in the spring flying along miles of hedgerow, you will suddenly see it dip, pause for a mere second, and then fly on. It has found a buckthorn, laid an egg on a prominent shoot, and departed.

It is not difficult to get ripe berries from buckthorn (which are small and black) and sow these in pots in the spring. Young bushes can be planted in suitable places with the co-operation of land owners, but these bushes really need to be 2 ft (60 cm) or more in size. The reason for this is that since they are scarce, the butterflies will lay too many eggs on them. The Brimstone female usually lays a single egg but it will fly on to look elsewhere, and since they are great travellers and live for a long period, the chances are that the same female will pass the same spot again and lay another egg.

Too many eggs will not only wipe out your small seedling but there will be insufficient food for all the larvae to reach maturity. Nature does provide some assistance, for the Brimstone larvae will find themselves overcrowded and will nibble each other, causing bleeding and death which will reduce their numbers. They do not actually eat each other.

Rhamnus frangula, the softer-leaved species, is also easily grown from seed, and in fact is very much faster growing. This species is removed from large areas when conifers are planted or when woodland undergrowth is cut for the benefit of other timbers. It never gets very large and the Brimstone will fly into quite densely wooded areas to find it. Anybody can grow these bushes and plant them at the edges of woodland rides (clear of mechanical ride cutters), and the result on the butterfly population is immediate.

When working on parasite research before the war, in the Chiddingfold area, I planted a great many seedlings. Not many years later one could stand anywhere in a ride and count a dozen male Brimstone butterflies without moving about. Ultimately conifers gained the ascendancy and eliminated most of these bushes.

The Orange-tip butterfly chiefly lays its eggs on hedge mustard, also called 'Jack-by-the-hedge'. It will also lay in the open on the cuckoo flower in wet places, but here it does not do as well since the larvae have a long way to travel before they can pupate in a safe place for the winter. Both the Brimstone and Orange-tip are unfortunately single brooded.

The Orange-tip is under pressure, not only from the removal of hedges, against which the food plant grows, but from mechanical roadside verge cutters which are usually operated when the growth is at its height in June and the worst possible time for the larvae of the butterfly. The cuckoo flower is still common in many places but as drainage progresses it will become scarcer. The seeds of hedge mustard are simple to collect and they should be scattered well in towards the base of hedges on the sunny sides of roads. When well back, the seed may escape cutters. You should scatter a few seeds at intervals over a long distance. The butterfly likes flying long distances down roadsides and dotting an egg or two here and there. Unfortunately the seeds take two years to mature to a flowering plant but any work of this nature that can be carried out will be of great assistance to this very pretty species.

I have been working in recent years on the rather scarce Glanville Fritillary on the Isle of Wight, the southern shores of the Isle of Wight being the only habitat in the British Isles where this butterfly is found. It feeds on plantain, chiefly the ribwort plantain, and there is no doubt that it likes the sight and smell of the sea. It will go right down to the beach in places. The colonies are threatened by cliff falls – not so much real falls but slides of clay and sand which obliterate the food. The little indentations of the coastline get covered with vegetation and give shelter from winds, providing suitable habitats for the butterflies to rest and lay their eggs.

The first stage of the work in increasing this butterfly was to examine the largest colony for parasites. There used to be an *Apanteles* species on this butterfly but it was not specific and also parasitized the Marsh Fritillary. Now that the Marsh Fritillary has gone from the island, the parasite may well have gone with it. Certainly I have not found it in the last eight years. While this search was being carried out it was possible to release all imagines bred out and these were placed in sheltered, isolated spots along the cliff. The new colonies thrived but then the trouble was lack of food. Starving caterpillars had to be moved elsewhere and some even had to be taken into captivity for breeding out. This problem is being solved by planting more food and by sowing more seeds. The chief threats to the species now come from earth movements, increasing numbers of people unwittingly walking and sitting about in these areas, and in the dry spring of 1970 a fungus disease attacked and killed a number of larvae. I also suspect that the large numbers of jackdaws, which now go unchecked on the cliffs, are not entirely blameless. They will descend in a mob and clear an area of most insect life.

An active group or body such as the Isle of Wight Natural

STUDYING INSECTS

History and Archaeological Society will give a great deal of help towards preserving this interesting species so that it can continue year after year without a lapse.

It will be seen from these instances that practical conservation as applied to entomology is fairly simple in a great number of cases. The scientific information required is almost all in books of reference and it is a matter of knowing what species are available in an area and looking to see that their needs are met on a permanent basis.

The White Admiral may well disappear owing to the great change in modern woodland husbandry. This butterfly prefers to ignore clumps of honeysuckle and lay on wisps of honeysuckle twining round slim poles in a wood. The female flies right in amongst the trees to find the right places.

Today cutting copses for poles every five years or so is too expensive and there is also a change in demand for the faggots and poles. This practice used to be ideal and such woodlands were abundant with the White Admiral. You used to get a small twist of honeysuckle round every pole and larvae on each one. Now the woods are denser, the honeysuckle goes higher to get the light, and of course the planting of solid conifers kills off everything.

In a case of this sort there is little that can be done towards conservation of a particular species. It will linger on along rides, finding the odd suitable place here and there. The trouble will come when for some other reason, such as mild winters or wet weather during mating and laying time, the species in a given area will be hit and then, since the numbers are already low, it will disappear altogether. The introduction of a number of females into a fresh area is a great help to a species of this sort and I consider a great deal more of this type of work should be done. In the past it has been very much frowned upon by entomologists who have made careful lists of species in their district. It upsets their records. Where such mobile animals as insects are concerned, the value of such lists might be in question and I think it is high time some collectors got their sense of values right. In times past, a small but very beautiful butterfly was introduced into this country. Feeding on nettle, it actually got established until it was deliberately collected to the point of extermination by a well-known entomologist because, as he said, it would upset his records.

The actual introduction of species to a new area requires care, particularly with butterflies, since not only must you satisfy

CONSERVATION

yourself that the habitat is quite suitable but the specimens to be released must also be selected with care. In the case of butterflies, you should not select absolutely fresh specimens but those that are slightly worn. By this means you will be sure to take fertilized females and although they may have already laid some of their eggs, this is a safer plan than to risk robbing a district of a freshly emerged female and taking it where there are no males of the same species.

Butterflies, such as the Chalk Hill Blue, mate almost as soon as the female has hatched, and indeed you can sometimes see males pairing with a freshly emerged female while she is still trying to dry her wings. It is easy to place a large net over a pair of these and wait until they have separated. You then box only the female. If you take both, the males will go on chasing the females and interfere with their attempts to lay eggs. Likewise, if you box two butterflies when they are paired you may cause premature separation and the eggs then laid may not be fertile. Worse still, the female will often not mate again. This is particularly the case with moths.

Another butterfly which lends itself to being transferred to a new district and which will do well is the Marbled White, but you must be quite certain it will be in a suitable place. This butterfly is chiefly a limestone district species, liking downland and open spaces. Recently I have introduced it to woodland rides where there were only conifers at the sides and I have several large colonies doing well. It was only necessary to introduce a mere three or four females. I think they have done well because the sites are sheltered from high winds. So often on the open hills these butterflies get blown about a great deal and take refuge by getting into the longest grass they can find and sitting tight. As their life-span as an imago is not very long, this cannot be good for them. The pretty little Speckled Wood butterfly is another species which is easily transferred. It is in no danger at the moment but it is not found everywhere and there is no reason why more woodlands should not be colonized by this attractive species.

These general principles of conservation can be practised anywhere in the country where they apply, but it must be emphasized that correct information must first be obtained before anything is tried out. I was once told by a large landowner who had some fine woods, including many oak trees, that he was expecting to see the Purple Emperor butterfly; he had plenty of sallow ready,

STUDYING INSECTS

and he hoped the butterflies would multiply under his protection. He certainly had a considerable amount of sallow, the narrow-leaved variety, all growing in a swampy area and never likely to be visited by that butterfly.

Under my direction he planted some broad, soft-leaved sallows along the edges of wide rides, well back, so that a big oak would partly shade them. It was three years before the Purple Emperors were there in sufficient numbers to be noticed. They did well but, even so, artificial aid from man was still necessary. Every year about half of each sallow would be pruned right back hard. The time chosen was when the butterflies were just appearing. In case any pupae were still on branches which were cut, these were left in a bunch against the bush and removed much later on. In this way vigorous growth of fresh sallow was produced and this was invariably selected by the females when laying their eggs.

Most of this chapter has been about butterflies, chiefly because, being more visible, they are more interesting to cultivate and you can actually see the results. There is nothing I like better than to see a few male Brimstones in the spring and to know that I may have had a hand in their appearance.

The conservation of moths is easier since they are very much more adaptable than butterflies. A much greater proportion of moths will feed on more than one plant and many species are omnivorous. Only those species that are highly specialized by having either rare food plants or breeding only in the most impossible of situations require special attention, although some would appear impossible to assist. Such a species is the Isle of Wight Wave. This only occurs on the cliffs on the western point of the island. On the cliffs is an understatement – over the cliffs is better. The chalk here is very high and almost perpendicular. Here and there a very slight slope occurs, impossible, fortunately, to climb on, and this slope will just support thin vegetation, and it is in this situation the moth is found. In the past, collectors have rolled stones over the cliffs to dislodge the moths which are then blown upwards by the air currents almost always found in such situations. I cannot see anyone condoning hacking away the cliff-tops to make more slopes for vegetation. However, nature and erosion does this at its own pace and unless there is a most unfortunate and extensive series of cliff falls, this little species will still carry on.

Fortunately today far fewer collectors specialize in this group of the Geometridae and those who do so are much more interested in

CONSERVATION

the insects' welfare and leave them alone so that they can still hang on – literally! How could you help a species of this sort? Possibly by moving it to more favourable slopes such as those below the lighthouse at Swanage, but in this case the numbers are so few that it would be extremely dangerous to remove living specimens. This is an example of an impossible situation and fortunately there are not a great many of these difficult species. Those species that are restricted to one particular kind of food plant are easier to consider. Their scarcity is not always due to the encroachments of mankind. Pause to think for a moment and see if you can remember where you have seen an aspen tree. This is not a rare tree and will grow on a range of soils from clay to sand. Without this tree you cannot get the pretty little Light Orange Underwing (*Archiearis notha*). It will feed on nothing else, and the aspen is not a tree that would readily come to mind when planting a copse. Actually the moth prefers a clump of aspens in the open or on the edge of woods. The general public are not likely to see this species, for it is about too early in the year, flying high up when the trees have no leaves and only a few catkins. However, if we are to consider conservation we must, I think, take a very wide view, so that first principles apply, namely, to see that large areas of natural countryside are preserved and with a very wide range of plant growth, and making sure that over the years the balance of things do not alter. Additions to the flora can follow later.

One of the chief points of present-day conservation, which must be watched all the time, is that of water-levels in marshy districts. In Wood Walton Fen, already mentioned, Lord Rothschild built himself a bungalow right in the fen, standing on concrete piles which went through some 12 ft (3·6 m) or possibly more of wet peat, on to firmer ground below. The fen itself was never drained, but of course there are dykes to take off surplus water in times of flood. Unfortunately, extensive agricultural drainage has taken place, much of it many miles away, and the water drains out through the thick peat. Lord Rothschild could skate away in winter, from the bungalow steps. Now you can almost walk upright under the bungalow. The peat shrinks as the water recedes and not only does the top dry out but the whole character of the area alters. Reeds give way to sallow bushes and in time will become wood. It takes much time and labour to keep an area as large as this in anything like its natural state, and I think The Nature Conservancy here will in time lose the battle. It would not be outrageously expensive to dig a trench with a mechanical digger, right round a huge area, down to the clay which underlies the peat. If this clay was dug as well, a bank could be lined with it, thus giving a watertight basin, and this would maintain the marsh plants and insects. When last I visited the area there was talk of digging, but this was to make a large pond for birds. To an entomologist, birds seem to receive more than their fair share of attention from the nature-loving public as a whole!

When Dr Blair discovered his Wainscot moth (*Sedina büttneri*) on the marshes at Freshwater, Isle of Wight, there were a great many there and it appeared to be a strong colony. Then two things happened at the same time. Collectors went down to the marsh and caught all they could find of this species, which was new to this country. The moth had no real chance either to multiply or possibly to find and adapt to different foods. This might have taken time but it could have happened. Then the local authorities decided to try and drain the marsh. The food plant of this new species was *Carex acutiformis*, a marsh plant requiring a considerable amount of water. Protests were made, but while they were being made digging went on and the water was lowered sufficiently to kill the plant and wipe out the moth. The area today is designated as an area to be preserved, but the water-level is still far too low. The reeds are drying out and have even become a fire risk.

This is a classic example of where about 2 ft (60 cm) of water would have made all the difference. I have mentioned that, at the time of writing, farmers get paid by the government to remove hedgerows. They also get paid for filling in ponds, so it looks as if insects who thrive on marsh and water plants are in for a thin time unless more people become aware of the great need for conservation in certain areas before it is too late.

Such is the concern in this country of responsible bodies of entomologists over the increasing loss of natural habitats and the resultant decrease in British insect fauna that, in March 1972, it was thought necessary to publish a code for collecting which entomologists are asked to follow in the cause of conservation. This code, under the title *A Code for Insect Collecting*, was drawn up by the Joint Committee for the Conservation of British Insects, and published in *The Entomologist* by the Royal Entomological Society of London. It is printed in full in this book in Appendix I, p. 135.

Insect Classification

Basically an insect belongs to that great group which is known as the invertebrate animals, that is to say, it has no skeleton inside but has soft internal structures with hard parts on the outside for protection.

An insect in the adult stage is defined as having a head, a thorax, to which its three pairs of legs are attached, and an abdomen or tail; it usually possesses one or two pairs of wings.

The various kinds of insects fall into fairly convenient groups which have been called orders. For the purpose of classification and naming insects, these orders are divided into super-families and families. The families are divided into genera and each genus into species. The wings serve to distinguish the genus in most cases. If you wish to take a serious look at insects, it is as well to be able to recognize to what order an insect belongs, for this will at least enable you to look it up in the correct book.

The reason for separating insects into various orders is partly due to their structure and partly due to their method of development, in which, of course, structure plays an important part.

The most obvious order for the beginner to examine is that of the Lepidoptera, which covers all the butterflies and moths. There is virtually nothing to separate butterflies from moths when their structure is examined. They both have four wings. Moths have serrated or 'fluffy'-looking antennae and butterflies have a simple, thin, hairlike structure with a knob on the end. One group of moths, the Burnet family, also have very similar antennae, but these sit with their wings flat, and not raised up and closed together like those of a butterfly when at rest. To confuse matters the geometrid family of moths can all sit with their wings up like those of a butterfly, but nearly all geometrids fly only at night. Moths have probably developed their habit of flying at night as a means of survival from attack by birds.

STUDYING INSECTS

The life cycle of the members of the order Lepidoptera consists of an egg, a caterpillar or larva, a chrysalis or pupa, and an adult insect or imago. The time of year that these changes take place is of no importance as far as their classification is concerned. Abroad, in a continuously warm climate, one insect brood follows another but in colder climates, where there is not the warmth or the food available in winter, insects have evolved a variety of methods of surviving the cold weather. Some stay dormant during the winter and this can happen during any of their four stages. The less clever ones try and fly back to warmer climates and many species just die out from the cold and we rely on fresh migrations from overseas before we can see them again.

Structurally, the most important part of the order Lepidoptera is that of the pupae. These are formed inside the skin of the larva and when ready for development the larval skin splits and slides off, leaving a soft pupa which soon hardens. The moth or butterfly grows inside this pupa and when it emerges as an adult it leaves the whole case behind.

If you look at another large and well-known order, that of the Coleoptera, which covers the beetles, there are structural differences which separate this order from the others.

Beetles must be familiar to all. They include the black beetles found under stones in the garden, cockchafers or may-bugs, wire-worms, glow-worms, scarabs and ladybirds, to mention only a few.

Their life history is much the same as that of the order Lepidoptera. There are the four stages of egg, larva, pupa and adult, but there are obvious differences in structure which can be easily examined. The adult beetles have the same four wings, but the front pair have been modified and hardened into elytra or wing cases, which protect the lower wings when the beetle is not flying. Flying is achieved entirely by the lower pair of wings.

The Coleoptera pupae are even more distinctive. Here the larval skin does not slide off but the larva gradually becomes dormant and assumes the shape of the beetle to come. The legs form, and these are external as they would be in the adult and are not enclosed in a smooth outer casing as in a moth pupa.

Some moths form a cocoon of silk or other substances which is merely an outer case for the protection of their pupa and is not a living part of themselves, and a few beetles also make a similar structure though much more primitive.

INSECT CLASSIFICATION

In the order Diptera, which includes house-flies, mosquitoes, daddy-long-legs, hover flies and midges, the life cycle is again in four stages but their structure differs from the two preceding orders. On examination of any of the above flies you will see they have only one pair of wings. One pair (the lower ones) have either vanished or been modified into two knobs used for balance while in flight.

Diptera larvae are also distinct, for they have no legs. Some can progress by wriggling about and some have short hairs or bristles placed in rings on the body which aid their progression.

Here again the larvae do not shed their skin to reveal a pupa, but gradually shorten and harden into a pupal stage. Once having achieved this, however, the next stage is different again since they break out like one of the Lepidoptera and leave behind an empty pupal shell.

Another large order to be found in this country is that of the Hymenoptera which includes ants, bees, wasps, saw-flies, ichneumon and braconid flies and gall-making wasps.

In this order we return to four wings again. In the autumn flies often come into houses and they are extremely like honey bees. If you examine one closely you will see at once that it is not a bee or a Hymenopteran but one of the Diptera, since it has only two wings. You can then become reassured and pick it up in your fingers.

The Hymenoptera again have the four stages of development and their larva are also legless like those of the Diptera. Their pupal stage takes place inside a thin cocoon which they construct, and this is like that of the moths and is not an integral part of the insect. In the case of the bees and wasps, the cocoon consists of a cell occupied by the larva and then, when the right moment comes, it is sealed over with a silken cap by the attendant workers in the hive or nest.

If you wish to examine the life cycle of one of the Hymenoptera you cannot do better than dig up a wasp's nest. Here you will have all the four stages at the same time. Some cells will have eggs just inside, placed there by the queen. Other cells will contain larvae and others will be capped over and when opened will reveal pupae in various stages of development, from quite white to the colour of the adult wasp. The pupal stages resemble those of the Coleoptera, with external legs, and they gradually darken to become adult wasps, when they eat their own way out through the cell capping. Their wings are soft and have to harden before flight takes place, and it may be a day or two before they leave the nest (Plate 16, below).

The ichneumon flies of the order Hymenoptera act as parasites of the various stages of the other orders of insects. They are more commonly found when you attempt to look after caterpillars of moths and butterflies which have been collected in the wild state and not obtained from eggs laid by an insect in captivity. With the exception of a few species, chiefly those found feeding among batches of spiders' eggs, the larvae of the ichneumon flies all feed internally in the bodies of their various hosts.

The braconid flies behave in much the same way as the ichneumon flies but this order is one which has a very great number of different species. They are separated on account of a structural difference. Remembering that an insect has a head, thorax and abdomen, in braconids the first segment of the abdomen, that nearest the thorax, has in the distant past been transferred to the end of the thorax. We can tell this because along each side of the abdomen is a pair of spiracles to each segment. These are apertures connected with the breathing system. Not only does a braconid abdomen have a pair of spiracles missing, but the end of the thorax, to which the missing segment was transferred, shows the pair of spiracles.

So far we have dealt briefly with the insect orders whose life cycle develops in four stages. There are, however, some orders where the basic life cycle is quite different, as we shall see in the following examples.

Dragonflies, or Odonata as the order is called, all lay eggs. The next stage is not that of the caterpillar – it is quite different. The Odonata have a stage called a nymph when they look like a very small version of the adult insect but without wings – these it will grow at the last skin change. The nymph has prominent legs (three pairs) and it can change its skin like caterpillars of other orders. It does not pupate however. When fully grown, the nymph crawls from the water to a reed stem or something to which it can fasten itself. It then bursts open at the thorax and the adult dragonfly crawls out and hangs to the stem to allow the wings to develop and to become hard enough to permit flight. Dragonflies often fly about with their wings still slightly soft. The adult legs come out from inside the legs of the cast nymphal jacket, and it can be seen that this cast jacket was part of the living insect, for at the opening where it bursts there are always white threads which once formed the

INSECT CLASSIFICATION

attachments to the internal parts, now moved away as a dragonfly.

The adult dragonfly has four wings and although there are distinctive forms with short fat bodies or long thin ones, it might be considered the easiest order to recognize.

A rather similar order is that of the Orthoptera which includes the grasshoppers and locusts. Again we have eggs and nymphal stages but the last nymphal stage is quite different. It does not alter in one burst as in the case of the dragonfly nymph, but develops wings to become an adult grasshopper. The grasshoppers all have four wings but the front pair are more like those of the beetles. They are hardened and serve to protect not only the hind wings but the soft abdomen as well. In this case, however, they differ from the beetles. The beetles carry their front pair of wings, or elytra, up out of the way of the active hind wings. The grasshoppers can use their toughened front pair of wings to aid their flight. At one time this order included the stick insects and leaf insects (which occur abroad) and cockroaches and mantids. These are now divided up and new orders have been created so that the cockroaches now come under the order Dictyoptera. Their life cycle is much the same as that of the grasshoppers, with egg, nymphal stage, and a winged adult stage.

The earwigs (or ear-wings) have the order Dermaptera all to themselves and they need no description here. Their life cycle is a very simple one of eggs and nymphs, while in the final adult stage a pair of wings is folded under very short and soft elytra. The wings fold up like a fan and then in half so that they are short enough to fit under the short elytra. It will surprise you if you manage to unfold one with a fine pin.

Another group with an order to themselves is the caddis-flies, who belong to the order Trichoptera. These are often first seen in childhood when you dabble in ponds and find their larval cases made from small bits of wood or plant remains cemented together. It is quite a large order with species across the world and their life history is more like that of the Lepidoptera with four stages of development. The pupa, however, has external or free legs and is formed inside the larval case. The wings and antennae are also free from the pupa and the pupa itself can be mobile, which enables it to reach the surface before emergence of the adult takes place. The adults look very like moths with harder-looking front wings and softer and paler hind wings.

The last order of any size is that of the Hemiptera which

includes all the 'bugs'. All these were formerly grouped together but as knowledge progressed they were divided into sub-orders.

The Hemiptera include the plant bugs, which are fairly soft-bodied, rather compact insects, but easily distinguished by their long, pointed mouth-parts, generally tucked away below their heads and which are used for sucking the juices of plants on which they feed. Cicadas, of which only one species is found in England (Plate 4, above), belong to one of the sub-orders. The well-known greenflies or aphids are also included in this large sub-order as are the frog-hoppers. These are more easily known from their larvae which make the well-known blobs of cuckoo-spit produced by sucking juice from plants and blowing bubbles with it. They then conceal themselves under it.

Another sub-order of the Hemiptera includes insects such as the Water Stick Insect, the Bed Bug, fortunately now scarce in this country, pentatomid bugs, which can stink when handled roughly, and the slightly better known water boatmen and water scorpions. The order still consists of a variety of insects living in quite different ways and they will probably be divided up again when much more is known about them.

Altogether there are now thirty-one different orders of insects, some being found only in hot climates and many only being represented by quite a small number of different species of insect. They are all listed below except six which are either extremely small insects, or very difficult to recognize, or only found in the tropics.

In the scientific classification on pp. 17–18 the most primitive order is given first, that is to say, the insects which have evolved the least since life began, and the list ends with the most advanced, considered to be the Coleoptera or beetles.

The more primitive insects are harder to recognize unless they thrust themselves under one's nose as it were. The very first order includes the bristle-tails and quite a number of houses will, at one time or another, have been inhabited by the Lepisma or Silver-fish, found on kitchen floors, near heating systems, and generally at night. They are quite harmless and scavenge on waste cereal matter.

INSECT CLASSIFICATION
INSECT ORDERS

Thysanura	Bristle-tails or Silver-fish
Collembola	Spring-tails. Exceedingly small, found under rotting plant material and visible when they jump
Ephemeroptera	Mayflies. These are the 'flies' copied by fishermen
Odonata	Dragonflies and demoiselle flies
Plecoptera	Stoneflies. An aquatic group found crawling over stones under fresh water
Orthoptera	Grasshoppers, locusts, crickets
Phasmids	Stick and leaf insects, including the stick insects used in the schoolrooms
Dermaptera	Earwigs or earwings
Dictyoptera	Cockroaches and mantids
Isoptera	Termites or white ants
Psocoptera	Booklice. Minute insects often seen among books and papers in houses
Mallophaga	Lice. Commonly found on birds
Siphuncula	Lice. Including those found on humans
Hemiptera	Plant bugs
Hemiptera	Sub-order: Homoptera. Cicadas, tree-hoppers, frog-hoppers, aphids
Hemiptera	Sub-order: Heteroptera. Water stick insects, bed bugs, water scorpions and water boatmen
Thysanoptera	Thrips. Extremely small but well known to gardeners
Neuroptera	Alder flies, lacewings, which are small delicate green insects with shining eyes, often seen in the autumn when they enter houses to hibernate. Ant lions, found on the Continent and in warmer countries, and looking very much like dragonflies but with antennae
Mecoptera	Scorpion flies. A small group; English adults having four wings about an inch across, with square spots. Can be seen sitting on brambles in the shade
Lepidoptera	Butterflies and moths

STUDYING INSECTS

Trichoptera	Caddis-flies
Diptera	Two-winged flies, such as the house-fly, mosquitoes, etc.
Siphonaptera	Fleas
Hymenoptera	Bees, wasps, ants, saw-flies, ichneumon flies and gall wasps
Coleoptera	Beetles

Insect Structure:

DEVELOPMENT AND FUNCTIONS

Even if you only intend to study insects in the field and look at their behaviour and life cycles, it is necessary to know a little about their basic structure. However, there is a lot more to it than just knowing their three parts: head, thorax and abdomen. Insects have been on this earth for a very long time and during this time they have diversified and evolved. In addition, there is the fact that most insects can produce one generation a year, and a great many species can manage continuous broods and have many generations in a short space of time. There are some exceptions which take several years to mature, but these are few.

The ability of insects to have many broods means that evolution can be speeded up considerably and, in fact, with certain insects we have been able to observe evolution actually taking place in a matter of a few years. This means that diversification and modification can take place rapidly, and it is possible to have insects belonging to a single order which at first glance seem poles apart and not in the slightest way related. It is not until you examine their structure, and sometimes even their internal structures, that the true relationship becomes apparent.

Insects have adapted their various parts to such an extent that it is important to know why a part has developed in a particular way if you are to understand the true functions of that part. This will also help you to understand what occurs in the field when you study the biology of insects.

Wasps and ichneumon flies belong to the same order, and the queen wasp and ichneumon fly will both lay eggs but the fly lays its egg inside a host, not loose. It will thus require a longer egg-laying tube and has developed one over the years. The *Rhyssa* species of the parasitic ichneumon fly, however, needs to lay an egg in or very

STUDYING INSECTS

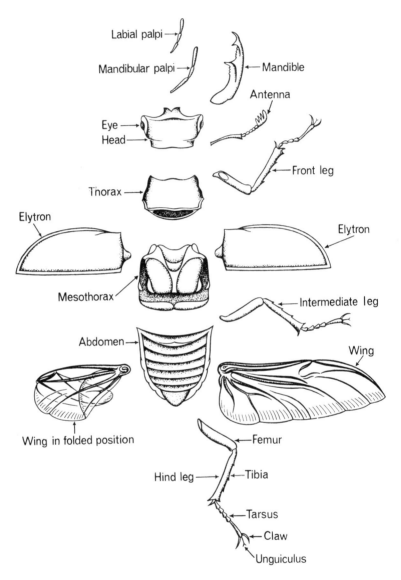

Fig. 1 Anatomy of a Stag-beetle

near the grub of the Sirex Wood Wasp, which may be right inside the trunk of a pine-tree. The ovipositor in this case is almost 3 in. (76 mm) long and special methods are employed by this fly to thread it in between the cells which form the solid wood of the pine trunk. Thus when you see an insect in the field equipped with this sort of weapon, you will at once have some idea of what its habits are going to be.

The head of an insect does not vary a great deal, but certain parts of it do. To take an example, if dragonflies had small eyes they would fall very easy victims to birds and the adult dragonfly also hunts for food while on the wing. Dragonflies, however, have been in existence since the carboniferous age so they have had plenty of time to evolve their eyes and they have developed huge eyes, almost as large as their thorax, giving them all-round vision and thus great advantages. Try approaching one at rest and see for yourself.

The development of most insects takes place during the larval stages when the feeding takes place. If, however, as is the case with some insects, the adult also feeds, then modifications are required for their mouth-parts according to their diet. A Convolvulus Hawk moth will feed right inside trumpet-shaped flowers, so it has developed an extremely long tongue or proboscis. A locust will eat all manner of vegetable matter, so its jaws or mandibles have grown very strong and efficient.

A male stag-beetle, however, does not require food as an adult but has adapted its jaws in the manner of a stag's antlers and uses them for scrapping with other males. The mandibles of the female are left quite small.

In the tropics many males of the beetle family have very spectacular jaws, or horns as they have become. In some the function appears to be lost, or they have become merely decorative and might even serve to impress females. Others have huge jaws but lined with soft hairs. These are used for seizing a female and carrying her away – not only from other males, for when you consider that grass and herbage is over a foot high, it must be quite a feat to find your female, and once having done this you would not want to lose her again.

Besides the development of the tongue and mandibles, there is that of the sensory organs or 'feelers'. The stag-beetles have two pairs, a labial palpi associated with the tongue and a mandible palpi associated with the jaws. These are required by insects for examining their food, and in some cases for detecting the correct plant on which to lay their eggs.

Butterflies and moths possess antennae which are feelers placed immediately behind their head. In the case of dragonflies and the order Diptera, these have been reduced to mere bristles since these insects have superior eyesight.

Moth antennae, especially those of the males, have evolved over the years, and a simple way to distinguish between the sexes is by the very simple antennae which the females possess compared to that of the males who have larger and more complicated structures. These enable a male to detect the scent of a female over great distances.

Butterflies make a great play with their antennae before mating will take place, but they use their feet to detect food. If you find a hibernating butterfly in the house when it wakes up in the spring, you can get a small pad of wet cotton wool and sprinkle a little sugar on it. When the butterfly's feet touch this, it will uncurl its tongue and start to feed.

The thorax of butterflies and moths is a simple affair, and the two pairs of wings and their three pairs of legs are all attached to it. In some orders, however, the thorax has been developed, and although it looks one unit, it will divide into three parts, or segments, called a prothorax, mesothorax and metathorax. In this case one pair of legs is attached to each segment, but a pair of wings attached only to the mesothorax and metathorax.

Some insects have no wings, for having ceased to use them, they have become obsolete and in time disappeared. Some female moths have only the vestigial remains of wings but the winged males can fly to them. Queen ants are born with wings but bite them off when they start a nest underground since wings would get in their way.

Some insects' legs have been developed to extremes. The Mole Cricket has much enlarged front legs, enabling it to burrow into the soil.

Worker bees have a place on their hind legs in which they can store pollen. Insects' legs are not used merely for walking. They take the place of hands in humans. The joints, where the elbows would be in a human, have short, strong, pointed processes or protuberances. These are used as combs, particularly for wiping sticky pollen grains off the antennae and from the hairs and scales on their wings, for which the back legs are used. Insects are regarded as 'dirty', an unfair comment since they are most particular and spend long periods performing their toilet; if they didn't do this they would soon get gummed up and be unable to move about.

The tail or abdomen of an insect has also been subject to adaptations. Some dragonflies like to oviposit in water so their tails have been greatly lengthened to enable them to do this without getting wet. It also enables them to balance the light weight of the rest of the body to make flight feasible.

Earwigs have developed forceps on the end of their bodies as a defence mechanism. Besides making them look dangerous, which is a very great asset, earwigs can give a slight nip with them as well.

In many cases merely possessing some feature which looks formidable affords an insect protection from either other insects or birds.

The abdomen is divided into ten or twelve segments but these are not always visible and are hard to count since some segments have been altered or transferred to the thorax. In some cases, segments have been adapted for uses inside the end of the body, for example, to hold eggs, as in the cockroach, or as parts of their egg-laying mechanisms.

Dragonflies can grip their opposite sex with the ends of their tails during their mating. The glow-worm beetles have developed lights in their tails to attract others, and of course there are many other examples of structural adaptation − in the stings of insects, the range of ovipositors of parasitic flies, and not least of all the saws used by saw-flies to slit open a leaf into which they can insert their ovipositor and lay an egg in a safe place. If you have some idea of what these various adaptations in an insect mean, you will be able to learn a little of what takes place during their life. In fact it has, in some cases, only been possible to find out the reason for a particular piece of insect apparatus by observations made with the living insects in the field.

The Perfect Insect

CATCHING

Butterflies

You cannot easily catch a flying butterfly without some sort of net. True, in my schooldays I caught a Blackveined White in a school cap without a great deal of harm to the specimen, but a net is better.

One might suppose that inventing a net would be easy, but early collectors struggled with a 'bat fouler'. This comprised two poles like hockey sticks covered with netting. The intention at first was to approach ivy-covered walls at night, clap the poles against the ivy and then work them together, thus entangling roosting sparrows. The curved ends stopped them coming out at the top. One also caught the occasional bat – hence the name. Early entomologists used this device for catching butterflies and there is a good illustration of one in Moses Harris's *Aurelian* dated 1760, but it was not until about 1890 that a round net appeared in William Watkins's catalogue of equipment. Plate 3 (above) shows some early collectors with a bat fouler about the turn of the century.

Early entomologists were considered a little mad. Their storage boxes, for instance, were designed to look like learned leather-bound books. William Watkins even listed an 'Umbrella, with case and spring, causing it to be fitted at a moment from an apparent umbrella to a complete net – 7/6d.' A clever idea, but it was possibly madder to be seen out in pouring rain with your umbrella folded than in sunshine with a butterfly net in use, so this net became obsolete.

Today the best net for general use is the kite net, a pear-shaped net with a brass socket handle into which can be fitted, if required, a stick of some sort. The chief advantages of this net are that it can be more easily used without a stick, being just about the right length to reach to the ground, and that the widest part is furthest away from you, just where you want it.

THE PERFECT INSECT

There are times when you must have a long stick, such as when collecting off a tall bush or working on a steep bank, but for running about in a field I think the shorter the handle the better. There is also a round folding net, generally with three hinges – one opposite the handle, one at each side; since the handle is detachable it is often called a 'four joint' net. There is also a very handy little net called a spring steel net, where the frame is made of steel strip; though about 12 in. (30 cm) across when in use it folds up to about 3 in. (8 cm) and fits easily into one's pocket. I have often carried one when doing something else and have been able to whip it out quickly and catch a passing butterfly.

A simpler net is one with a Y-piece of brass or some other metal at the handle end and a length of pliable cane bent round and stuck in. The chief disadvantage of the simpler nets is that they will not fold away into a satchel – an important consideration for the cyclist. The beginner can make a cheap net by taking a thick piece of galvanized wire and twisting it on to a handle of some sort, first threading on the bag part. All things considered it is better to buy a net than struggle with an inefficient home-made one.

Butterfly netting is best made of plain cotton and not nylon, the specimens being more perfect when caught with the softer, more

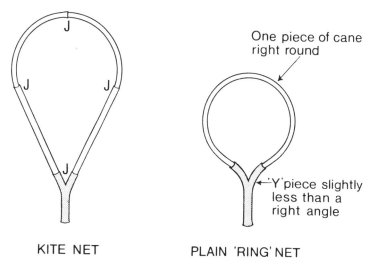

Fig. 2

yielding material. When making netting, manufacturers use a 'dressing' which leaves it crisp and fairly stiff. Without this it would be almost impossible to cut and machine into net bags and other articles. When they first receive a new net bag, collectors think it too harsh for delicate butterflies, but the dressing soon wears off. It can be removed by washing, but I do not advise this as netting shrinks more than you would expect. You can rub the netting in your hands to hasten the process, but a few days' use in the open air soon softens it, and once in the right condition it will always remain so. This explains why you may think nylon netting is softer when you see it alongside cotton in shops, and may be tempted to buy what I think is the wrong material.

Black netting is better than white. Insects appear more visible to some people through green netting bags, but the greater number of collectors prefer black.

A net bag should be the length of your arm when reaching in to box a specimen. You can then hold the net in one hand and box or bottle your capture with the other without having to lay the net on the ground and fumble with too much netting, which will damage your specimen. An arm's length will also allow sufficient netting to fold over the frame to retain a specimen in the bag for examination. This means that if you catch a butterfly and twist the net the bag will fold once round the frame leaving a small portion free in which the specimen is trapped. You can see how this is done from the photograph on Plate 3 (right).

When catching insects on blackberry blossom, you should shake out the bag to its fullest length and then tuck the extreme tip between the third and fourth fingers of the hand holding the net. If you make a stroke at an insect sitting on a bramble you should release this tip just after the net has passed the bramble and the specimen has entered the rim. The bag will then straighten out and the insect pass into the end. Failing this the tip will wrap itself round the bramble branch and you will watch the specimen fly away and probably tear your net as well.

When catching a butterfly or other insect which is on the ground or on a low flower you should make a sideways stroke and not bang the net down on top. If you do you may break your net and will almost certainly miss your specimen as the net bag will fall in a tangle and you will not be able to make a second stroke; but if you strike sideways you can always do a quick swerve if the insect changes direction.

THE PERFECT INSECT

If you see a butterfly coming down a woodland ride, don't stand like a goalkeeper in the middle of the track, but get in to one side and use an overtaking shot. Otherwise a Brimstone will very easily dodge you.

One method of catching butterflies which does not require a net at all is the 'grass stalking' method. Chalk Hill Blues and a number of other species roost on long grass at the foot of the hills and if possible in a place out of the wind. They roost gregariously, that is to say several on one stalk. Stand with your back to the sun and walk slowly forwards and you can examine them as you go. Once in Wales I saw some long grass in a corner of a field protected by low stone walls. A pole lying across the corner prevented cattle from eating right into it. Roosting there out of the wind were over two hundred Small Copper butterflies. They would scatter far and wide during the day and then gradually collect as dusk began.

A good many years ago, when the Purple Emperor was a little more common and rabbits certainly were, it was the practice of collectors to bait for these beautiful butterflies. The method was to kill and paunch a rabbit and then lay it on a log or tree stump. Male Purple Emperors are attracted but I think females prefer a damp patch of ground which they visit just before the sun gets low. Of course you cannot just put a rabbit out and wait. It takes a day or two for the butterflies to find the lure and another day for them to get used to visiting the spot. Sometimes damaged oak trunks ooze sap and this can be most attractive to the Red Admiral. These butterflies are also very fond of feeding from ripe plums on the ground. Although this is about all you can do with baiting in this country it is the best method of catching butterflies in the tropics, and in many places the only one. The method is to watch animal droppings which will attract a great many species of butterfly. Some collectors have also tried various fruits in a fermented state but with very varied results.

In the hotter countries a trap can be made for butterflies. This is a simple contrivance made from two square wooden frames with a long pole at each corner making a tall oblong box about 5 ft (1·5 m) high. The poles should be left protruding at the bottom end so that these can be pushed into the soil. The whole is covered in netting except the frame at the base, which is left open. The base should be about 3 in. (8 cm) up from the ground level, and on the ground under the square frame the bait, such as rotting fruit or animal droppings, is placed.

STUDYING INSECTS

This trap operates on the principle that when a butterfly leaves the bait it will fly upwards, and when it finds itself confined it will continue to fly upwards. A black cloth over the upper third of the cage might allow butterflies to sit quietly and not damage themselves. On the other hand it might cause them to fly downwards and out.

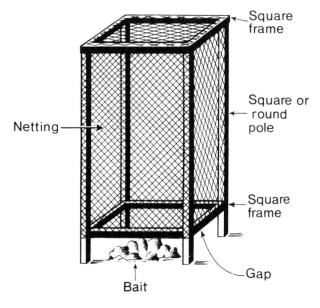

Fig. 3 Butterfly-trap used in tropical countries

A few words may be added here on catching dragonflies. Never make a wild pass at a dragonfly. Keep still and watch it flying up and down; it may even pass extremely close to you. Wait for this and immediately it passes make a stroke to overtake it and you will catch it easily. The huge eyes and superb eyesight of dragonflies enable them to dodge nets easily when seen head on.

Moths

Moths are, if anything, more rewarding to study than butterflies. To begin with there are many more of them, both in kinds and in numbers, and you may follow the chase all the year round and not just when the sun is shining.

THE PERFECT INSECT

There are certain moths which will fly in the sunshine just as butterflies will. The Cinnabar moth, a bright red species flying amongst ragwort, is one of these and also members of the Burnet family. The Fox moth does a violent flight, almost uncatchable, low over the heather in the middle of the afternoon, but night is the time when things really get going, and about 1 a.m. the best time of all.

The ideal way to see moths at night is by using a mercury vapour trap. Unfortunately these are rather expensive but there are no short cuts. The bulb and choke are both costly items which cannot be dispensed with. The numbers of insects on some nights, however, are phenomenal and have to be seen to be believed.

An M.V. trap (Plate 7, below) consists of a large base with a transparent cone on the top into which fits an inverted plastic cone holding the bulb. There is a grid below to allow water trapped by the plastic cone to escape through the base of the trap.

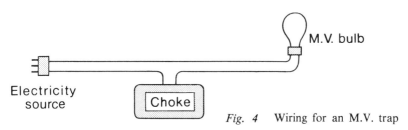

Fig. 4   Wiring for an M.V. trap

M.V. bulbs are fitted with three-pin sockets to prevent one from placing them into an ordinary socket. They need to warm up before taking the full strength of the current, and a choke is inserted in the circuit for this purpose. It is best to have the choke indoors and run a lead of plastic-covered flex down the garden to a suitable open space. The more open this space is the better, for moths are quite happy to sit on a brightly illuminated fence without progressing nearer the trap.

Those flying round the bulb strike a vane on the plastic cone and enter the trap. It is best to line the inside of the base with half-sheets of egg-packing card. This is placed on edge round the sides and greatly increases the surface on which the moths can roost without damaging themselves. The trap can be left on all night at a negligible running cost. In the morning you can lift off the lid and examine the sheets of card; on a good night each indentation will hold several moths. The great interest of this method is that with many moths of one kind you are likely to get a variation in their markings as well as a number of different species. Unwanted moths on the card should be tipped out amongst tall foliage; if you tip them out on the lawn the birds will eat the moths. It is very important to take proper care of unwanted specimens from traps. If you tip out moths as instructed you should have no trouble, but sometimes at a given date you may find you have too many large Yellow Underwing moths. These are very powerful flyers and also very active in a trap, so they are inclined to flutter wildly about and damage other specimens. This is why egg-packing material is useful, since moths can take refuge in the many indentations and sit quietly. When you get an overdose of Yellow Underwings you could take these right away before liberating them. Some people use an anaesthetic in an M.V. trap to render the moths stationary for easy examination. This is not a good practice, for a percentage of the catch will be killed.

For densely built-up areas, to avoid inconvenience to neighbours, a dark-coloured bulb (Wood's glass envelope) is available, which, although emitting the essential ultra-violet light, shows only a faint purplish glow. These dark bulbs, having thick glass, crack in rain, and cannot be left out in wet weather. The ordinary M.V. lamp has relatively thin glass and so is not liable to crack. However, damage by rain can be prevented by using a transparent disc mounted above, as shown in Plate 7 (below). If you have only one house near by and the occupants are not too friendly you can place a tin disc on a short stick close to your trap and this will throw a shadow over the house without unduly affecting your catch.

You can now buy a household type of light bulb incorporating M.V. and this is manufactured by Philips. It plugs in like an ordinary light bulb and does not have a choke. The principle is that it incorporates an extra filament of the usual type. This heats up when the bulb is switched on and then the M.V. part comes into play. While many times better for moth catching than a normal filament bulb, it has however nothing like the effectiveness of the proper M.V. bulbs.

Incidentally, if you switch off an M.V. bulb and then put it on again it will not light. Don't think you have broken it; it will have to cool down for a few minutes and then will relight gradually, which is why these bulbs are not suitable for household use.

There have been many attempts to find a good portable lamp incorporating M.V. lights but so far this has proved very difficult. A number of collectors now use a 6-watt actinic tube which is lit from a 12-volt car or dry battery. This however requires a ballast unit placed in circuit and it is really best to go to a good electrician to get this properly connected.

One of these tubes can be stood in a standard trap and if you fasten it low enough there is no need to modify the vanes on the cone.

This method gives out a certain amount of ultra violet light but you lose between 60 and 70 per cent of the catch which would be obtainable with a standard Robinson type M.V. trap. In other words you do little better than you would do with a good incandescent petrol or paraffin lamp on a sheet.

Fig. 5   Tilley incandescent collecting lamp

I have seen collectors use a spare car battery and have a switch in the car. Once you have set out on a journey you can switch over to the spare battery and thus put it on charge for a time and repeat the process on the return journey. This type of lamp will run a car battery down fairly fast, when in use.

The perfect answer is a good generator but the cost is fairly high. I prefer to use a long cable and connect to the nearest house. After all there are generally buildings not too far away. You should remember moths will fly long distances although a few species hardly fly at all, but these can be found by other methods.

If you cannot afford an M.V. outfit you can have good results with an ordinary electric light or, in the field, with a paraffin or petrol incandescent lamp. These work well but you have to remember that they may only be effective on certain nights, such as

STUDYING INSECTS

warm, still, thundery ones. There will be nights when you will not see anything while on the same night an M.V. trap may be working wonders. The incandescent lamps are ideal for searching for larvae at night.

There are a few tips to remember when using an incandescent lamp. You should always filter your fuel into the tank with a filter funnel. This applies to electric generator sets as well. This funnel will remove any water or fine grit. It only takes an extremely fine piece of dirt to block the fuel jet, and struggling with one of these on a dark night is not to be recommended.

Always carry a spare mantle. You might damage one in transit or even poke it with a long grass stalk. If you use a mantle with a small hole or crack in it you will find a jet of hot gas will come out of this under pressure and heat one side of your glass globe, and later this will crack. Although heat-proof glass is used this only works if heated evenly.

If used without a trap a lamp is best with a white sheet placed flat on the ground. The lamp can be stood on a box or stone to raise it slightly. This works well in woods. In open country such as marshes you should look for a little hump-backed bridge over a dyke. These often have gates across them, so hang your sheet on the gate and place the light in front.

There are many ways of seeing moths. You can plant a buddleia bush in your garden; several, pruned at different dates, will give you a constant supply of bloom. Examine these with a torch at night and moths will be feeding on the blossom. A red light will not disturb them and you can inspect them at leisure.

Another and most effective method is that of sugaring. To a base of molasses or black treacle are added various ingredients according to your own whims. The main essentials are something to give the mixture body – the treacle or molasses, something to attract, and alcohol to make the moths dopey and less likely to fly off when you try to box them. The best attraction is the essence of the jargonelle pear, which is hard to buy and most expensive. A good substitute is amyl acetate or 'pear drops', which is very cheap and can be bought at any chemist's. Then you can add rum or slightly fermented beer. If you are in any doubt about what to do, just buy a tin of black treacle and remove four full tablespoonfuls. Add to these two tablespoonsfuls of methylated spirit and one teaspoonful of amyl acetate and stir well. Keep the lid on until you are ready to try it out.

THE PERFECT INSECT

Of course not all nights are good sugar nights: you need a warm muggy night with little wind. You can select a line of posts or a row of trees along the edge of a wood, and on these you paint a strip of the mixture about 1 in. (2 cm) wide and about 1 ft (30 cm) long. You start when it is nearly dusk and by the time you have finished the last strip it will be time to return to the first and have a look at the catch. In one of the fens where there are few trees a line of posts is erected on each of which is nailed a lump of cork bark; these are often so impregnated by other collectors that you need only look at them!

On a good night moths will be elbowing one another off the strip trying to get at it, but I have had many blank nights, especially late or early in the year when it suddenly turns cold and almost freezes and nothing will stir. The great advantage of this method over the various other ways of attracting moths is that you will always get females as well as males so that you can obtain eggs and breed a series. The proportion of females to males coming to lamps is very much smaller if lights other than mercury vapour are used.

Nature has its own way of sugaring for moths by means of honey-dew, the sticky sweet secretion exuded by aphis flies which drips down from some trees such as limes and forms a shiny film on the lower leaves. This substance is attractive to most moths and if you see any about it is well worth a visit at night with a torch, but don't forget the moths may be a little more active and not drunk, so take your net along and tap them in rather than attempt to box your specimen.

The boxes are usually glass-topped and specially made for the purpose; these are rather expensive. Plastic ones are cheaper but not quite so good; since the sides are slightly shiny the specimens do not grip them so well and this makes them flutter instead of sitting still. Always keep full boxes of butterflies and moths in the dark. This type of box is not good for caterpillars since you will require a tin or something moisture tight to keep food fresh.

Assembling moths

This is a most exciting way of seeing moths, especially if you use one of those species which will perform nicely in the middle of the afternoon and not at night. The Oak Eggar is by far the best of these and to assemble this you will need to breed a few moths in order to be certain of getting a female. You can do this from wild collected larvae, but you will have to be most careful not to get these too warm or forced along too quickly or you will make your attempt when the wild stock is still in the pupa stage and nothing will fly to your female.

Having got your female – and you must of course keep it away from any males you may breed – you make a roomy muslin bag for it and hang this up about 6 ft (1·8 m) off the ground in a suitable area – the place in fact where you found your original larvae.

About three o'clock in the afternoon, if it is a warm fine day, the female will 'call'. This means she will climb to the top of the cage and hang down. She will then extrude a small organ from the tip of her abdomen from which will emerge a pungent scent, undetectable by the human nostril. This will waft away on the breeze and males will pick it up and arrive at full speed, sometimes in hundreds, from distances of up to two miles.

The Emperor moth will also react in this way. Mark a few males with that bright quick-drying fluid which is used in offices to correct stencils, and take these about two miles down wind in a car. Then get back to your female and see how many return and the time taken.

Apart from these daytime species, which are interesting if you have the time to watch them, nearly all moths will do the same thing at night and you can easily make a trap for this purpose. This consists of a perforated zinc tube about 8 in. (20 cm) across and 18 in. (45 cm) long. At one end you make a perforated zinc funnel or cone turned inwards and with a hole in the end about 1 in. (2 cm) across. The other end of the tube is covered by muslin or netting held in place by an elastic band.

You place your virgin female in a muslin bag as before and put this in the end of your tube opposite the funnel. You then hang the apparatus up about 6 ft (1·8 m) from the ground and align it so that the wind blows from the female towards the funnel end. In the morning you should have a number of males trapped and you can select a good one for breeding. This can be left in a large cage with the female the next night, but do not leave the cage where the sun will heat it. Some moths stay paired for twenty-four hours and might get disturbed and separate; this sometimes ends in infertile eggs and the female will not always pair again.

Another way to obtain adult moths is to wait for a calm day after a very blustery night such as you often get in July. Many moths, especially the microlepidoptera, will come down from the trees and sit on a fence along the edge of a wood for shelter, and examining these fences is a rewarding exercise. You should also look on fences under street lamps, since moths which have collected there will often remain until the following evening.

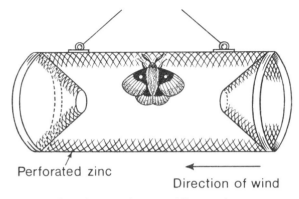

Perforated zinc

← Direction of wind

Fig. 6 Trap for assembling moths

Old oak fence palings, particularly if these are anywhere near a poplar or willow tree, are ideal roosting places for the Red Underwing. You should look along the fence early in the morning in early August: they will move off when the sun gets very bright. They should be put in a box or wooden tub with muslin stretched across the top. A damp piece of cotton wool sprinkled with sugar is placed on the netting for food and the females will lay their small grey eggs on the part of the netting which has become damp from the wool. Incidentally, never use treacle or honey as food, only pure sugar, as this keeps insects alive longer than other substances. The eggs will not hatch until the following year, when you can breed them right through. This is an ideal species for the beginner since overwintering is one of the great problems with some species and those which pass the winter as pupae or eggs are the best to breed.

Adult microlepidoptera

There are several ways of finding the adult small moth apart from catching in a net – although a net is used at the last minute in the examples I give below – and I think you will find these well worth trying. The first is the smoking method. You can use either cigarette or pipe smoke or buy a small bee smoker which employs a little roll or tube of corrugated cardboard. This is a good instrument but rather bulky to carry around on a trip. A much neater item of equipment is one invented by my late father, L. T. Ford, who was undoubtedly one of the greatest micro experts of all time. This gadget is merely the handle, with the tube part joined to it, of an old bicycle pump. When removed from the outer casing of the pump the tube is exactly the right length and the smooth handle makes an ideal mouthpiece.

The method of using this is to insert it into the base of a large grass tuft or clump and blow smoke in. This can be done in the winter months when you get hibernating moths and other insects. The faster moving occupants of a grass clump leave first – lizards, flies of various sorts, then moths and finally beetles which have to crawl up stems instead of running and flying. One of the chief occupants of the grass tufts will be the Gelechia family of micros. Plate 2 (below) shows a bee-smoker in use, a 'must' if you are a non-smoker.

The second very productive method of hunting concerns another group of micros, the *Depressaria* genus. You can collect these any time after the beginning of the autumn and even into late spring by holding your kite net bag taut across the frame and using it as a beating tray. You then tap along the edge of thatch on a haystack, or roof if sufficiently low, and the moths drop on to the net. They can generally be boxed easily but if they take to flight, or something more active or larger comes out, you have your net handy. Another very good place to try is reed thatching, especially if this is low down. You sometimes come across this in marshes and fens where it is used for small boat shelters or even animal shelters; it is extremely productive.

Certain pine-feeding moths may be caught by jarring the tree trunk, a method which works for other species as well. At first sight this does not appear possible, but a tree up to 6 in. (15 cm) in diameter may be jarred by a firm kick about 3 ft (90 cm) from the ground.

On a very windy day I once stationed a friend about a hundred yards down wind from a clump of aspen. He wanted to see the Light Orange Underwing, not a rare species but occurring in small localized areas. He stood there with a kite net in each hand looking as if he were trying to land a plane on an aircraft carrier, with the net bags standing out straight in the wind. I kicked the aspen trunks in turn but he swore he saw nothing, only leaves whistling past. Yet there were three moths in one bag and two in the other, and he had never even moved.

Other insects

One of the best ways of finding adult insects is that of sweeping. It is quite useless for butterflies or moths as it only results in damaged specimens. A kite net is used but with a white linen bag instead of netting, which would be caught on sticks and become torn. The method is the same as that used for sweeping larvae or beetles except that there is no need to brush herbage quite so hard and flowers will produce better results than plain herbage.

There are two quite different methods of dealing with the catch. The first is to place the net bag on the ground with the tail end

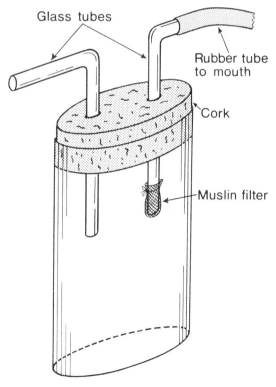

Fig. 7 Pocket pooter

towards the sun. The bulk of the insects caught will generally go towards that end and you can then put your head in the frame end and examine the catch. Small insects such as the smaller Hymenoptera and Diptera may be caught with a pooter, a miniature vacuum cleaner worked with a bulb or better still with your mouth. A sharp intake of air picks up an insect which may be $\frac{1}{2}$ in. (12 mm) away from the end of your picking-up tube. Flies caught in this way are subject to one great disadvantage, that they will sometimes be smothered in pollen from all the flowers. The way to overcome this is to keep your specimens alive in the pooter, which may be kept in the dark in a cool place. The insects will then carefully clean themselves of pollen and also of moth scales by brushing with their legs. It is quite an interesting process to watch and takes some time, for they are very thorough. When this is completed a small amount of killing fluid fumes may be carefully sucked in, or alternatively a small bead of cotton wool may be dipped in ethyl acetate and placed in the end of the tube. A little air may then be withdrawn which will allow the whole container to be filled with the anaesthetic.

One disadvantage of this method is that fast-flying flies will leave the net as you attempt to peep in, and you may happen to be looking for some of these. Another disadvantage – and one which weighs heavily with myself – is that sometimes there is a netful of angry hive bees amongst the catch and putting one's head amongst them can be far from pleasant!

Although you can release some of these quickly and still retain the bulk of your catch a better plan is to make a few quick strokes with the net and then, when most of the catch is forced by air into the extremity of the bag, close your hand round the end of the bag a little way up to trap the catch and lower it into a fairly large tin. In the tin you can have a pad of wool on to which you have dripped your anaesthetic. Hold the lid in place for a few moments until the buzzing stops and then turn the whole catch out on to a card tray. I advise a deep side to the tray in case you are at work on a windy day. You can remove anything you want with fine-pointed forceps or your pooter.

Specimens may be placed in convenient boxes, such as card ointment boxes. These need not have glass lids since you will already have sorted out the catch and only insects you wish to keep and kill will be boxed. These will recover after a very short time and, like those in the pooter, will start to brush themselves clean at

THE PERFECT INSECT

once. The remainder on the tray will start coming to life almost before you have finished sorting.

If you sweep for anything other than Lepidoptera, it is a sound idea to have special boxes marked 'NOT FOR MOTHS', and keep these for swept material. Normal boxes used for any kind of specimen will soon contain loose scales from moths. These get among the hairs of such things as very small Hymenoptera and are a perfect nuisance under the microscope, when they mask what you want to see, and have to be removed individually with a camel's-hair brush.

This style of sampling gives you a very quick and comprehensive picture of the type of insect found in a given habitat. You will get Hymenoptera and also numerous Diptera, Hemiptera, Homoptera, as well as Coleoptera. You will soon learn the difference in results to be obtained from sweeping over different plants or bushes, and when you become experienced you will find that no two persons going over the same ground will get the same results. One person may have a slightly longer reach and so brush a little lower or with more strength, while another may subconsciously be attracted by certain flowers.

When you return home after a field trip the card boxes are placed lid upwards on the table. You can then make a pinhole in any of the lids which do not have one already and with a small brush dab a drop of killing agent over the hole. This will stupefy the insects which can then be tipped into a killing bottle for a longer period. It is better to transfer them with fine-pointed forceps if you have the time since this will leave behind any pollen grains the insects will have cleaned from themselves during the journey home.

The most attractive flowers to insects are the umbelliferous group such as cow parsley in the spring and later on hogweed and wild parsnip. These have small open flowers where the nectar is easily reached and are often crowded with insects. A gadget once in great favour and one still used by a number of specialists is the net forceps or scissors net. This consists of two round rings on hinged stems which have handles like scissors and are made in such a way that when closed the two rings lie in the same plane and come flat together. One ring is covered right across with white muslin and the other holds a fine muslin net bag. They are snapped shut over a flower blossom and the insect is then allowed to crawl to the tail end of the bag before the frame is drawn off the flower. If you are standing amongst a clump of flowers this little net often makes less disturbance and you can take what you require selectively instead of having to net bees, etc., which, as I have mentioned, can be a nuisance.

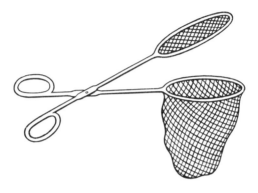

Fig. 8 Scissors net or net forceps for Hymenoptera and Diptera

A plant that is worth growing in the garden is the evergreen shrub *Bupleurum fruticosum* which will reach a height of three feet or more and has an attractive blue-green foliage with yellow umbelliferous type flowers. It is highly attractive to most insects, including Hymenoptera and Diptera by day and moths by night, but not to butterflies since these are first attracted by something colourful. The shrub is listed in the catalogues of leading nurserymen.

Lean-to glass roofs are often wonderful insect traps, especially if the lower edge rests on a wall forming a side to the trap. Diptera and Hymenoptera – though little else – are often caught in quite large numbers in this way. I once constructed some fine tubular traps for ichneumon flies using caterpillars as bait. They certainly worked but when I also caught a dragonfly and a bee or two I realized that any records of parasitism based on this trap would be quite unreliable! The insects fly in purely by chance.

For statistical records and research, flight traps are sometimes used; these are huge nets of fine muslin placed right across a woodland path. Unfortunately the correct weather is such an important factor when using these that they are not very successful in this country.

You can make yourself a very cheap and effective beetle trap by the following method. There are ready-to-cook pies on sale in tins

THE PERFECT INSECT

and these pie tins are ideal for making your own traps. You simply cut a circle out of the bottom of the tin (or a square hole if you prefer) to allow the beetles to enter, then solder a sheet of perforated zinc across the top edges and trim round. Turn it upside-down and it makes a perfect trap. The beetles can walk up the sloping sides and will fall in; the overhanging sides will prevent them from crawling out again, although some may fly out. If enough bait is present they are not likely to want to get out before you have had a chance of examining the trap.

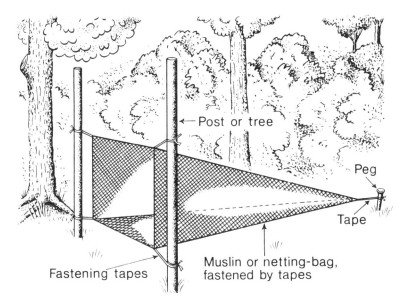

Fig. 9 Flight trap

These traps are exactly like the old 'black beetle' trap in use at the end of the Victorian era. (Black beetles of course were the common house cockroach and not beetles at all.) The old trap had a tin base, but out of doors perforated zinc is necessary for drainage.

The traps may be placed in a great variety of places; at the bottom of a hedge is often rewarding. The question of bait depends on what you are after. Over-ripe fruit attracts some species while beer or rum is attractive to others. Burying beetles are attracted by decaying meat and other related species by fox droppings, but this can be a subject for your own research.

I recently found a milk bottle standing almost upright at the edge of a wood. It contained some dark and very smelly matter in the bottom, which I assume was old milk, but it also contained two of the large black burying beetles, *Necrophorus humator,* and one of the orange and black banded species, *N. vespillo,* and a number of drowned Rove beetles. They were unable to climb out. It might be worth while to experiment with a pot of old Yoghurt as it looks as if this would make interesting bait.

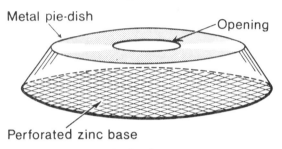

Fig. 10 Beetle trap

If you are looking for beetles examine flower blossoms, some of which are very attractive to certain species. Low-growing flowers such as the dandelion are often visited by several species of small bright green beetles. Hogweed growing along the edges of old woodland will produce the handsome bright yellow longhorns of the genus *Rhagium,* while the metallic green rose chafer can be caught, not on roses, but on the flower of elder bushes.

KILLING

Before you decide to kill any insect for study purposes you should make certain that it is one you really want and also that it is a perfect specimen, since it is a great waste to destroy a butterfly only to find it has a large piece missing from one wing and that it will have to be discarded.

Another point to remember, and one which is a little harder for a learner, is that it is silly to kill a female when you can keep it for eggs, breed a long fresh coloured series and let the surplus go. So often in the spring I have seen boys kill Red Admirals or Painted Ladies, newly arrived migrants from the Continent and more than likely females. They are the ones which will produce a brood or two if the weather is right, and become abundant towards the

THE PERFECT INSECT

autumn. The Clouded Yellow is another example which will suddenly become abundant towards the autumn if the first arrivals meet with favourable conditions. A later section describes how eggs may be obtained and managed.

You can kill a butterfly in an emergency by giving it a sharp pinch on the thorax, first holding it between the first finger and thumb from underneath, with the wings closed uppermost. It is impossible to succeed with a finger or thumb above the insect and one below; you will only damage the specimen. The disadvantage of the pinching method is that you need to become expert and nimble-fingered to do it well, without damaging the butterfly, and if it is not done effectively the specimen may partially recover.

The best killing bottle is a wide-necked jar into which are placed about three $\frac{1}{2}$-in. (12-mm) cubes of cyanide of potassium. These are covered with a layer of plaster of Paris. There is nothing to stop a chemist from making one of these cubes up for you if – according to the regulations governing the sale of certain poisons – you are known to him, and if of course you can persuade him to do the job. It is troublesome because of the plaster covering and it is worth little to him financially, so a busy man will try to discourage you.

The first thing to do when you get home is to take out the cork, place the jar on a high shelf for safety and get the plaster completely dried out, which will take only a few days. Then you can cork the bottle, allow the contents to get up strength for a day or two, and begin using them. If you don't do this they will 'sweat'. The condensation will contain cyanide which will form crystals on the side of the jar; this is dangerous, and your bottle will deteriorate rapidly. Always keep your bottle in the shade; keep the cork in when not in use and it will last five or six years. The plaster will turn pink or brownish a few days after you get the bottle.

Ammonia on cotton wool is a very effective killing agent but destroys the colours of many insects. Both carbon tetrachloride and ethyl acetate can also be used on a pad of cotton wool. There is a slight disadvantage in this since you may put in a little too much and an active moth may get under the wool and get wet which will cause the scales to mat. In the field the wool may also shake about. To avoid this you can put plaster of Paris in the bottom of your killing bottle and allow it to set and dry out and then use this to absorb whatever fluids you are using. Moths will, in the field, slide about on the surface so a little pad of cellulose tissue on the top helps to prevent this.

STUDYING INSECTS

Although carbon tetrachloride is a good killing agent, it leaves specimens hard. Perhaps the best method is to use the proprietary brands of killing fluid. These are made up with a mixture of chemicals to achieve a more rapid knock-out effect, so that an insect is killed before it has time to damage itself.

For killing beetles and insects which do not fly, plain ethyl acetate is ideal. It has the advantage of keeping the insects in a relaxed condition. It should never be used as an anaesthetic for either butterflies or moths, for it is far too slow in its action; a butterfly can flap a lot in the few extra seconds involved. Don't use chopped-up laurel leaves. Early pioneers used this for both killing and relaxing but it is too slow for killing Lepidoptera. Burnet moths cannot easily be killed in cyanide bottles as they are resistant to this chemical, so use an alternative; ethyl acetate could be used but it should be injected when it kills at once and leaves the specimen in a relaxed state.

Dragonflies should be stored alive in the dark for about twenty-four hours before killing, otherwise they will lose all their colour. They hawk up and down catching small insects as food and their bodies will be packed with the remains, which will decay when the insect is killed and turn it quite dark. If it is kept alive for a time, however, it will get rid of this food matter, and although the bright colouring may be lost you will certainly have the pattern markings to study.

The freeze-drying technique described on page 91 is particularly suitable for dragonflies. If they are preserved by this method there are two great advantages. Firstly the large eyes of the flies in the Aeschna family do not collapse inwards as is sometimes the case. This also happens with the Libellula species as well, but with all species of dragonfly the bodies keep their shape and almost all their colour as well.

Beetles may be killed with ethyl acetate, as already mentioned, but an alternative is to drop them into boiling water. This kills them instantly and they can then be mounted, but it sometimes causes their wings to open, and it is difficult to restore these to their natural folded position. After killing it is best to drain them off on blotting paper at once.

Green moths such as the Emeralds lose their colour and turn brown very easily. It is best to inject these with a small hypodermic syringe, using ethyl acetate. Although this chemical is too slow for killing moths when used as an anaesthetic, it is ideal for killing larger moths such as the hawks with a hypodermic. The method is to hold the insect between the finger and thumb and inject into the thorax from underneath using only a very tiny drop of fluid. In fact the plunger is hardly moved at all, slight pressure being all that is required. Early pioneers used to kill Emeralds with a mapping-pen dipped in oxalic acid.

Beginners may have a little trouble with butterflies which die 'inside out', i.e. with their wings folded downwards, instead of being folded in the natural way. This means that when the insect is lying in the bottle or relaxing tin the scales may become rubbed. To avoid this, take a pair of forceps and, as a butterfly becomes motionless, slip them between the wings from the head end to take hold of a leg. A gentle blow against the wings will cause them to spring back into the correct position and you should then lay the butterfly down in the bottle or tin and either place another specimen on top of it or a small piece of wool, which will keep it flat until it stiffens a few moments later.

RELAXING

If a butterfly or other insect is killed by a method other than one involving ethyl acetate it will stiffen after death. This prevents one from opening the wings to set it except by force. There is a natural period – some twelve to twenty-four hours after death – when this stiffness will disappear, but it is not easy to gauge this. The easy solution is to place the specimen in a relaxing tin, a flat tin with a suitable absorbent pad on the bottom and containing a commercial relaxing fluid. An alternative is plain boiled water, but it may turn specimens mouldy. Always remove any odd legs or parts of insects from your relaxing tin as these will turn mouldy in time and although hardly seen will act as a dangerous source of infection.

Specimens may be left in a relaxing tin for about twenty-four hours when they will be ready to set. If you are on holiday and want to store for a few days, use a second tin which is only just damp and then increase the fluid content when you get home. If you are abroad, and especially if you are flying and consequently travelling light, you can place specimens in a paper envelope with the wings folded. Suitable envelopes can be made very simply by folding a rectangular piece of paper of appropriate dimensions in the way shown in Fig. 11. Be sure to pencil the place and date of capture along one edge of the envelope. Ink is no use as it will run when you relax specimens later on. On reaching home you should lay these specimens in your relaxing tin, each with the cut-off data slip, for twenty-four hours. You should then pinch the thorax from underneath with your forceps, which will make the wings open a little. Then lay them back in the tin for a further twenty-four hours, when they should be ready to set. If they are still too stiff repeat the process. You can store these labelled insects in tins; add a little flaked naphthalene and seal up with some kind of plastic or surgical tape. Insects stored in this manner may be set a great many years afterwards. The same relaxing treatment serves to treat a specimen which has been in your cabinet and which you may wish to reset in a different style.

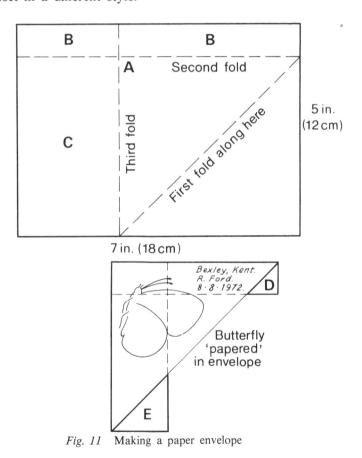

Fig. 11 Making a paper envelope

THE PERFECT INSECT

Very small moths or microlepidoptera are better relaxed in an old-fashioned zinc relaxing tin with cork on both sides. The tin is first scalded by water from a kettle and then allowed to drain almost dry. Pin the moths through the thorax shortly after killing and then pin them into the *top half* of the relaxing tin. To test for readiness you hold the pin in the forceps and gently blow on the

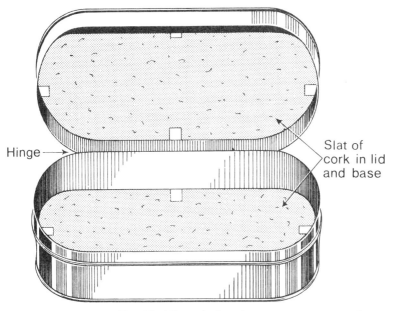

Fig. 12 Zinc relaxing tin

moths, when the wings should open. Avoid cotton wool which will entangle them and use blotting-paper on the bottom of your killing bottle. Blotting-paper also makes a good pad when you pin them out before placing them into the relaxing tin. If they are not pinned at this stage they will touch the damp cork and the fine fringes on the wings will become matted, which is why the upper half of the tin is used, for this allows the wings to droop down clear of the cork.

SETTING

This is quite a simple task but one which often deters the beginner because he does not understand the principles of relaxing. Once

STUDYING INSECTS

you appreciate these and do not attempt to set a stiffened insect the task is easy.

The first requirement is a setting board. This is a wooden slat covered with about ½ in. (12 mm) of compressed cork with a groove running down the centre and finally papered on the top. The widths of the boards are varied to accommodate the different sized butterflies and moths and the widths of the grooves are also varied, a wider one being required for moths and a wider one still for dragonflies and humble-bees.

With the setting boards you require some setting tapes or papers. These are transparent strips of paper of varying widths running the length of the board. Their purpose is to hold the wings in position until the insect dries out, when it can be taken off the board and will retain its position indefinitely if stored in a dry place. It is possible to use only one setting tape on each side if you are an expert but it is easier for a learner to use two on each side, one for holding the wings in position and a second for covering over the remaining parts of the wings (Fig. 13).

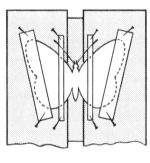

A
Strap method for single specimens

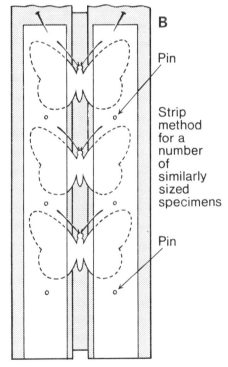

B
Pin

Strip method for a number of similarly sized specimens

Pin

Fig. 13 Methods of setting specimens

THE PERFECT INSECT

Proper insect pins are essential. The normal dressmaker's pin has a large head and often rusts. Entomological pins are made from brass, plated with nickel which leaves them 'white', or black enamelled. The choice is a matter of individual preference. There are better ones made from stainless steel, sometimes bluish in colour, and these are headless. You use a pin of appropriate length for the size of insect you have to set.

On the Continent the pins used are all 38 mm long and vary only in thickness. This means they can be long and thin and in fact springy. If you catch the top of one with forceps the head of an insect may fly off in one direction and the abdomen go in the other, and so you would be well advised to leave these pins alone. They were adopted years ago and it is too late to change, although many of the national museums on the Continent have now gone over to the English style of mounting the smaller Lepidoptera on a fine stainless-steel pin and passing this into a short bar of polyporus pith, rather like a matchstick, which is supported by a stouter pin carrying the data label, identification and registration number (Fig. 14). A further disadvantage of the continental style is that a pin of that length will not go into English style cabinets or on both sides of storeboxes unless these are specially made.

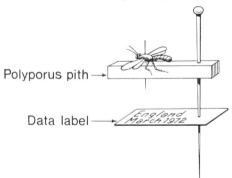

Fig. 14 Mounting a small insect on polyporus

You may see in older books pictures of rounded setting boards or saddlebacks, having sloping or rounded sides. Insects set on these have a drooping appearance, and this fashion became outdated many years ago. A board of this sort, however, is ideal for one purpose – a male Purple Emperor set in this way shows its purple colouring on both wings at once and looks superb. Set flat they do not catch the light rays properly to look their best.

STUDYING INSECTS

Also seen in old books are illustrations of the setting bristle or brace, a device to hold one pair of wings in position while those on the opposite side were set. These are not recommended as they often leave an unsightly mark on the wing and are cumbersome to use.

A chart of the sizes of English entomological pins is given below and against these the name of a well-known insect to give you a guide as to which size to select.

English Pins: Nickel-plated or Black

SIZE NO.	RECOM-MENDED LENGTH	INSECT
16	35 mm	Hawk moths (Sphingidae)
11	34 mm	Swallow-tails (Papilio)
12	30 mm	Vanessa
13	28 mm	Vanessa
5	25 mm	Smaller butterflies and Noctuids
7	23 mm	Geometers
8	20 mm	Blues (Lycaenidae)
9	15 mm	Pugs (Eupithecia)
20	15 mm	Now superseded by stainless-steel pins below

Headless Pins: Stainless Steel

DIAMETER	RECOM-MENDED LENGTH	INSECT
0.010"	15 mm	Pyralidae
0.0089"	10 mm	Tortricidae
0.0076"	10 mm	Tineina
0.0056"	10 mm	Nepticula

It is also an advantage to have with you a supply of Lill pins which are cheap to buy and which can be used to hold the setting tapes in position. These are also useful to hold carded specimens of beetles, etc., as will be explained further on. These Lill pins are only about $\frac{1}{2}$ in. (12 mm) long and so do not show very much when used for pinning carded specimens. It is advisable to use short pins to

THE PERFECT INSECT

hold setting tapes on the boards as these will not be so likely to catch in anything if you wish to pack the board away when travelling about. Very long pins will tangle with others when you close up a double-sided setting case holding boards on both sides (Plate 6, below).

There is a slight disadvantage for the beginner when using these pins in that you cannot easily hold them in your fingers and must use forceps. Forceps become second nature to the expert, but the beginner who does not wish to use them can use a box of glass-headed pins. These have large heads which enable you to handle them and push them in easily, but they will be long, which must be remembered if you wish to pack your boards away.

Fig. 15 Entomological forceps

Having decided on the length of pin you require, you should pin the specimen. Hold the butterfly with the wings closed between the finger and thumb of your left hand and then squeeze the thorax lightly. This will cause the wings to open slightly. You can then take the pin up in the forceps and push it through the centre of the thorax. The pin should be fixed in slightly forward since this makes setting very much easier (Fig. 16).

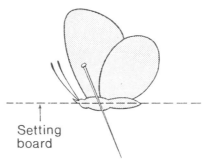

Fig. 16 Angle of pinning a butterfly through the thorax

Next you should fasten a setting tape on each side of the setting-board groove, as close as possible without overlapping the groove, and then raise these up out of the way over the top of the board.

STUDYING INSECTS

Pin the specimen on the board, taking care to see that the pin is in the centre of the groove and not leaning to the left or right, but with the head inclined slightly away from you towards the top of the board. You should at the same time take care to see that the thorax is the right height for the wings to lie flat on the boards when they are open and not bent near the body. This would either crack the main veins or cause the wings to 'spring' when the specimen was removed from the boards. When the boards are seen sideways, the pins should be all as in Fig. 16, and looked at end on, they should all appear as in Fig. 17. After finishing a board it is not a bad plan to check your setting style by looking at the boards in this manner.

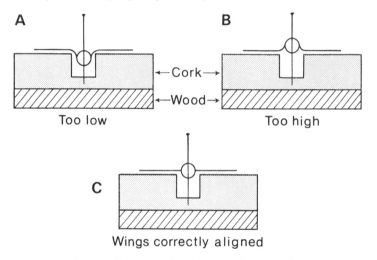

Fig. 17 Body position before setting the wings

Take a setting needle and lightly open the wings of the specimen; lower the tape on the right-hand side and pin this as shown in Fig. 19. This will hold one side while you raise the wings of the other. This is done by pushing the tip of the needle against a vein in the wings, the lower wing first and then the upper wing. As soon as you have the line formed by the junction of the upper wing with the lower at right angles to the line of the groove, lower the tape and secure with either one or two Lill pins above and below the specimen. Then release the opposite side and adjust the wings to match those of the other. The antennae should be held in position under the tapes.

I am inclined to favour a bent setting needle rather than a

straight one. If you slip off a vein when pushing a wing forward you will certainly pierce the wing and even tear it. If you use a curved needle in such a way that you drag it across the vein until you grip it, the movement will only be forward across the wing if it slips and not into the scales.

Fig. 18 Curved setting needle

Setting needles are supplied quite straight by the makers, but you can easily bend your own. Heat it near the centre over a spirit flame and when nearly red-hot bend it to the desired angle, which is about 135°, i.e. a right-angle and half as much again. This angle is rather important, but individuals may vary it to suit their own requirements.

I prefer to stand my setting boards upright once they have specimens on them. This enables the bodies of the insects to hang down and dry in a natural position. If the boards are left flat the bodies of the insects will often sag to the bottom of the groove and will dry in this position.

Some collectors make a small cupboard with shallow shelves on which they can store full setting boards, but these have the disadvantage of being flat. Boards left upright on the mantelshelf are apt to get knocked about when pins catch in a duster, and wasps have been known to attack the bodies of insects on setting boards.

You can make or buy a setting-board house, which is a box which opens out like a book and has boards in each side (Plate 6, below). The professional ones are made from japanned metal, which of course is termite proof when used abroad. The boards are held in position by a flange at each end. One end tucks under a ledge provided for the purpose and the other is held down by a removable bar. This enables you to remove the boards easily and to use boards of varying widths. The total width of boards on each side is generally 9 in. (23 cm). They can be laid flat when being filled, etc., and then stood upright like a book on a shelf when being stored. The insect bodies thus hang correctly as described.

The normal time allowed for drying is about three weeks as a minimum, and large-bodied moths take a little longer. When dried, the specimens can be removed to a storebox for sorting and labelling. Unless you use a setting-board house for storage during

STUDYING INSECTS

the drying, and one which contains an insect repellent such as flaked naphthalene, you should always transfer specimens into a storebox and not direct into a cabinet. This not only gives you time to sort and label them, but if an exposed board has been visited by mites or a museum beetle, any infection or attack will have time to show itself before you transfer trouble into a cabinet, where it might spread to valuable specimens.

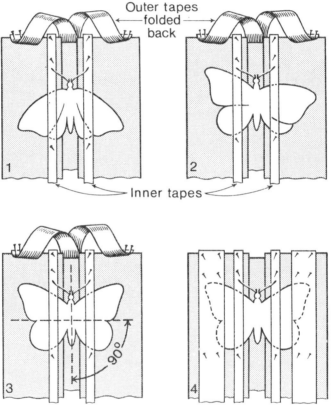

Fig. 19 Setting a butterfly

Insects on setting boards can be attacked by mice if within reach, by wasps if unduly exposed, by mites, certain clothes moths, and lastly by the museum beetle. The museum beetle adult is about the size and shape of the letter 'o' in this book. The adults can fly into a house and may lay eggs on insects exposed for drying. The young larvae can enter small crevices, so storage boxes should be

THE PERFECT INSECT

as tight fitting as possible. The larvae are very furry and change their skins several times. A larva may be feeding in a body or hidden under a wing so the cast skins may be the first sign of trouble. While flaked naphthalene will help to keep them away, you should use the crystals of paradichlorbenzene to kill the pests. These can be placed in a very small muslin bag pinned in one corner of your box. Good storeboxes have a camphor cell into which you place the naphthalene, while cabinets have a larger one for the same purpose. Should you overdo the quantity of naphthalene in your cabinet and your room has a sudden drop in temperature, the naphthalene may crystallize like frost on the wings and bodies of your specimens. If this happens don't attempt to remove the crystals. You simply take off the drawer lid and allow the naphthalene to evaporate, which may take twenty-four hours.

Mites are harder to see and the first sign of trouble is generally fine powder on the floor of the cabinet or storebox. On close examination you may see minute specks moving. Paradichlorbenzene will also kill these.

When you set the antennae of very small moths, they are often very fine and sometimes short or extremely long. If you mount a fine camel's-hair brush on the end of your setting needle, you can moisten the tip of this on your tongue and gently stroke the antennae, which will stick to the paper on the setting board long enough for you to get the setting strip over them to keep them in place.

MOUNTING

Many insects are set in the style used for butterflies. Dragonflies and others in this group, Diptera or two-winged flies, and even grasshoppers can be set in this style, although to save space it has been the custom to set grasshoppers on one side only, the other side having the wings in the resting position.

Beetles or Coleoptera are generally mounted on cards if they are small, or pinned through the right wing-case or elytra if they are large, and the legs kept in place by other pins until dry. When mounting beetles on cards you should adopt one or two rules to achieve a uniform and presentable collection. Cut your cards to a suitable range of sizes and keep to these. Don't try to mount the beetle on its final card at first, it is often too difficult. You should take some cheap card and using a cheap water-soluble glue or gum,

STUDYING INSECTS

mount the specimen with legs and antennae in a natural position using as much gum as you wish. Several specimens may be gummed on one card with enough space to separate them by cutting the card later on. After a few weeks' drying you may cut the card up and soak the pieces individually in a shallow saucer of water so as to loosen the card without disturbing the position of the legs. If you don't cut up the card it curls up and half the specimens are in the water and half out. A deep bowl is no use, for you would alter the positions of the legs when getting the specimens out. A camel's-hair brush will help in lifting the specimens clear and you may drain them for a moment on blotting-paper.

Next get your clean card, good Bristol board about the thickness of a good quality visiting card, and place on it a small drop of gum tragacanth containing a preservative as supplied by dealers for entomological purposes. This will secure the specimen and will be hidden by the thorax. There is no need to gum the legs which are already dried and in the correct position. This will give you a collection where the specimens are on clean card with no traces of excess gum that has turned dark brown or stained the card. It is customary to write the place and date of capture on the underside of the card, and a Lill pin placed centrally at the base of the card will pin the specimen in your cabinet.

Earwigs and many other insects may be treated in the same way. Although the larger Hymenoptera, such as the humble-bees and wasps, and the larger wild bees, such as the Andrena family, are set in the same manner as butterflies, on boards of appropriate size, the remaining groups of Hymenoptera are mounted in quite a different manner. The other groups in this huge order are mostly of very small insects, apart from the larger ichneumons, and a low-power binocular microscope is necessary to determine species in nearly every case.

This means that the specimens have to be specially mounted, and for the Microgasterinae, chalcids and insects of similar size the method is to gum on a card point as in Fig. 21. The tip of the

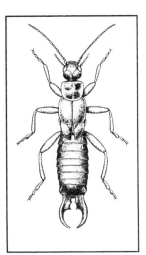

Fig. 20 Earwig mounted on card

THE PERFECT INSECT

point is touched with a little gum and the specimen to be mounted is then picked up with a camel's-hair brush and placed on the gum. The head should be to the right, the abdomen to the left, and the wings away from you. The gum should just touch the specimen on the thorax, behind the head and at the base of the wings. Care should be taken with these tiny insects not to fix them to the card point by just a leg. This is very easy to do if mounting with only the naked eye, and the leg will probably come off the specimen which will then be lost.

The pin is placed centrally through the square end of the card mount. If the pin is picked up by the right hand and held under a binocular microscope for examination, the head will be to the right and the point to the left; the specimen will then have its head away from you and you will be looking down on its back. This standardized method of mounting is of great assistance when examining specimens, since much identification is done by comparison. You must carry certain features of the specimen in your mind, and if you have the second specimen mounted in an unusual manner it is viewed from a different angle and so of course comparison is very difficult.

Fig. 21
Card point for mounting small flies

Care must be taken when picking up the specimens. The brush can be dampened with the tip of your tongue to make a fine point, but don't use a wet brush since it is essential to keep these small insects away from any damp which might mat the fine bristles or setae. Some collectors mount by using fine forceps. I am not in favour of this as it is very easy to damage setae on the wings; if you do use this method, handle the hind wings only as these seldom have characters used in keys for determination.

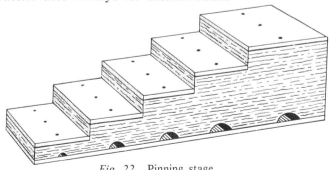

Fig. 22 Pinning stage

STUDYING INSECTS

The pinning stage is absolutely essential in this type of mounting (Fig. 22). This was first standardized by the British Museum (Natural History) and consists of a block of wood or wood covered in metal in the form of a low flight of steps; there are pin holes in each step which go right down to the base, where there is a metal stop. The card point is placed on the top step, the first data label on the second, and so on. The last label is usually a catalogue or registration number, or a determination label, giving the name of the species and the name of the person making the determination. This gives the whole collection a very uniform appearance, and if possible you should use a standard-length pin throughout, such as a No. 11 white (34 mm).

In addition to the pinning stage mentioned there is now an improved pattern on the market (Fig. 23). This has a flat top, but the depths of the holes vary. There is also a row of holes through the side which serve to show you the depth of the downward hole and to clear away fine paper fragments which might in time clog the base of the hole. This type of pinning stage enables a large card to be used as well as small points; these cards are sometimes essential for batches of parasitic cocoons or other objects. The improved type of stage gives exactly the same depths as the earlier model.

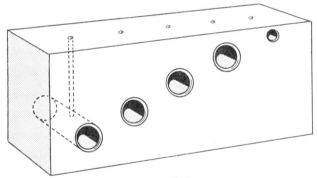

Fig. 23 Improved pinning stage

The pinning stage, as used in the Department of Entomology at the British Museum (Natural History), has the following measurements which are the same for both the old and the improved patterns. The measurements are those between the top of the stage (or shelf, as the case may be) and the metal at the bottom which prevents the pin from going down any further: 4 mm, 9 mm, 14 mm, 18 mm, 24 mm.

THE PERFECT INSECT

The private collector may not use all of these depths, but in the museum they were evolved by having a standard-length pin for specimens mounted on card points. The card, of course, is at the highest point. Next comes the label giving the country of origin, place and date of capture. If it is parasitic, the name of the host if known, or if not the method of capture, is recorded. Below this comes the identification of the species label and, lastly, the museum registration number (or your own reference number).

Using such a stage makes a great difference to the appearance of a collection, and if all labels are at regulation heights it also ensures that they can be read without being disturbed. Once a label is taken on or off, or moved about, it will work loose and always be out of place.

Breeding

THE EGG STAGE

Butterflies

Many of the British butterflies will lay eggs in captivity if given the right conditions and correct food plant. You should get a round wooden tub about 2 ft (60 cm) across and 18 in. (45 cm) high. Next you require two long thin withies from a hedge. Bend these as shown in the illustration and cover with netting or an old net bag, first mending any holes (Plate 7, above).

You will need a jar of flowers – kinds such as buddleia from which butterflies can get honey, not roses or lilies. This jar must not be too tall. One with a wide base, such as an office paste-pot or a horseradish-sauce jar, is the best, and your flowers must not touch the sides or top of the netting. If this happens the butterflies will trap themselves against it and will soon get battered. It is essential that they should be quite undamaged since they must reach the food plant, often to lay in special positions. If they are frustrated you will not get any eggs.

The next essential is of course the correct food plant. Small plants of nettle growing in flower-pots are good, especially if you snip back the long shoots and make them sprout more thickly.

The whole outfit is placed in the sun out of the wind and away from cats. The Orange-tip will lay well on hedge mustard, but keep changing the plant and don't get too many eggs on one stem or you will have trouble with the larvae later. This rule is a general one, except for those larvae which are naturally gregarious and feed in a web.

White Admirals will lay on honeysuckle but you must stick a large branch of leaves in the ground close by so that the sun filters through the leaves. The Silver-washed Fritillary will lay on muslin or netting hung round the sides of your tub and this should be removed and kept in a clean jar until the early spring, when you

BREEDING

can bring it into a hot room and force the larvae along on boxes of viola plants. You will then get fine sized larvae before the busy season starts.

You will only be successful if your butterflies have already mated before you catch them, so don't keep an obviously freshly emerged female. They won't pair well in a cage of this sort as in nature they often make special mating flights, and if you put males and females in together they may flutter too much and get damaged.

You should place a pad of cotton wool on the top of the netting and keep this moist with sugar and water to supplement the food. It is also a good practice to visit your cage during the heat of the day and sprinkle it lightly with water. Warning: never use treacle here.

Comma butterflies, and if you are lucky the Large Tortoiseshell, can be caught on the blackthorn blossom in the spring but will not lay immediately. The Large Tortoiseshell may wait six or eight weeks. You can keep them in the same type of cage if you keep the food going, but at this time of year you may get long cold, wet or dull spells of weather and they will be best kept indoors. You should then tame your butterfly and get it used to being fed artificially.

To do this you take your butterfly to a closed window. If it chooses to fly, it will go towards the light and you can catch it against the glass. Have ready a saucer and a wet pad of cotton wool on which you have sprinkled some sugar. You could try picking the butterfly up between the finger and thumb and gently standing it on the pad. Butterflies 'smell' with their feet, and often they will put out their tongue or proboscis and start probing for a drink as soon as their feet touch the wet wool. If they do not catch on to the idea at once, you can gently pick them up again and with a long, thin pin gently ease out the tongue by uncoiling it. When drawn in, it is coiled up like a watch-spring and by gently inserting the pin point towards the middle you can get it to stretch out. You then lower the butterfly on to the pad and let the tip of the tongue touch the wettest part; the butterfly will then start to feed. After a few moments it may stop and coil up its tongue again, and the wings will quiver. When this happens it will shortly take to flight so return it to its cage. Butterflies soon learn this feeding procedure and after a lesson or so will start to feed on their own.

The Clouded Yellow will lay well in captivity but as soon as you catch one you should go to your nearest corn stores and get $\frac{1}{2}$ lb

(226 g) of lucerne seed. A farmer might give you a little if you cannot buy any. Sow this thickly like mustard and cress in several seed boxes. The young larvae of the Clouded Yellow will romp on this food. No cage is needed, you simply place them on the boxes and keep them in a window. The old plants of lucerne are too tough by late August and you will only breed small larvae. By using the seed method you can obtain fine specimens which will go on hatching up to Christmas. If you cannot get lucerne plants for egg laying you can use clover, but it is not so attractive for the females.

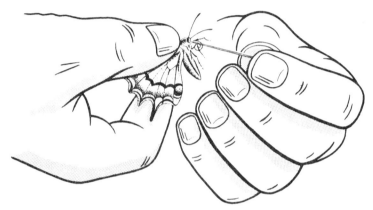

Fig. 24 Uncoiling the tongue of a butterfly for artificial feeding

Moths

Most moths also will lay in captivity and in fact they are very much more obliging than butterflies. No very elaborate cage is required to obtain eggs from species such as Lime, Poplar and Privet Hawks and Puss moths, to name only a few – a plain cardboard box is all you need. It must be deep enough for these larger species to move their wings and you must remember to have it reasonably caterpillar-tight since the young larvae will be very small when first emerging. A leaf of their food in the box will trap most of them as they hatch and you can transfer this leaf to your rearing cage when the larvae have crawled on to it. The Large Elephant Hawk, however, prefers to lay its eggs under the leaves of willow-herb or fire-weed, so you can place a jar of this in your box.

If you are in doubt about a species and cannot find a reference to its habits in a book, it is always a good plan to try fresh food

Examining the contents of a mercury vapour moth-trap

PLATE 1

Planting out young Cicada grubs

Using a kite net as a beating tray under thatch

PLATE 2

Smoking out adult microlepidoptera

(*above*) Early collectors with a 'bat-fouler' net in foreground

PLATE 3

(*right*) The end of a stroke with a kite net; the end of the bag is folded over to prevent insects from escaping

The only English Cicada, *Cicadetta montana*, from the New Forest

PLATE 4

Grub of the New Forest Cicada

(*above*) Burying Beetle, *Necrophorus vespillo*, on rabbit fur

PLATE 5

(*left*) Caddis-fly (adult) at rest on a rush

(*left*) Sugaring old tree-stumps

PLATE 6

(*below*) Wooden travelling setting-board case

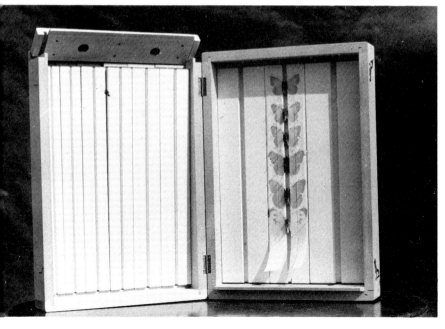

(*right*) Egg-laying tub ready for butterflies. Note sugar pad on top

PLATE 7

(*below*) An M.V. moth-trap assembled. The disc at the top keeps off direct rain and the knobs at the side enable it to be stood on its side when required

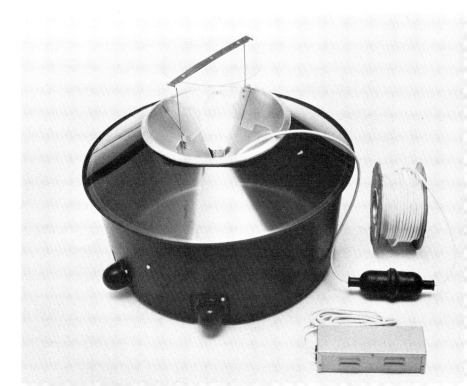

(*above*) Dor Beetle with mites clinging to its underside

PLATE 8

(*right*) Rose Chafer, *Cetonia aurata*, on an elder flower

Wood Wasp, female, *Sirex gigas*, ovipositing

PLATE 9

Grub of the Cockchafer Beetle

PLATE 10

(*above*) Placing sleeves for larvae on bushes. One is finished and tied at both ends

(*below*) Beating large trees with a sheet. The poles at each end make it easier to handle

(*above*) A folding beating tray (Bignall pattern)

PLATE 11

(*right, above and below*) Digging pupae at the base of a tree

Common Blue, female, *Polyommatus icarus*

PLATE 12

Cinnabar Moth, *Callimorpha jacobaeae*

Large Marsh Grasshopper, *Stethophyma grossum*

PLATE 13

Bush Cricket, *Tettigonia viridissima*

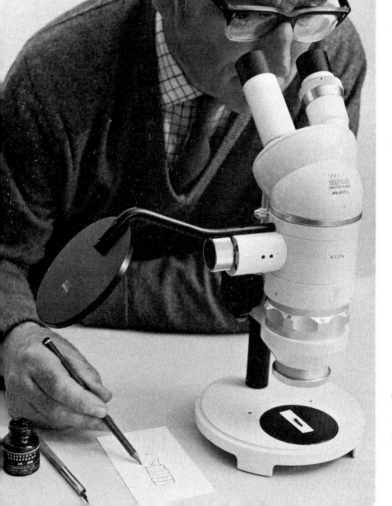

PLATE 14

(*above*) A battery of cylinder cages

(*left*) Using Wild microscope when drawing specimens

(*above*) Early form of microprojector

PLATE 15

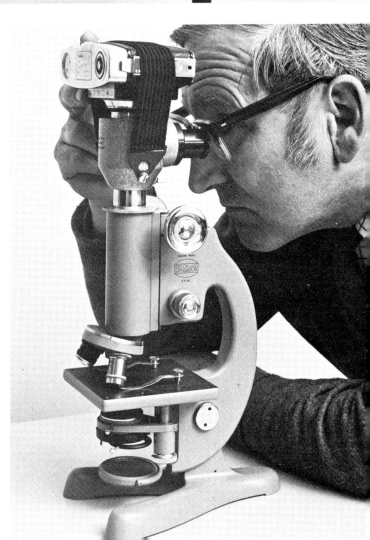

(*right*) Photographing specimens through the microscope

Bush Cricket, *Leptophytes punctatissima*

Wood Cricket, *Nemobius sylvestris*

PLATE 16

Bush Cricket, *Platycleis denticulata*

Tree Wasp, *Vespula sylvestris*, nest

BREEDING

plant first, then other attractions. Some moths will like a piece of rough bark so that they can tuck their eggs into crevices. The Lackey moth, however, will want a nice smooth twig and will lay its eggs in one tight ring right round it. Other species sometimes like pieces of rather old and teased-out string, and although all this may not be given in textbooks, getting unusual species to lay for you is part of the fun.

COLLECTING LARVAE

Butterflies

Many British butterflies may be found quite easily in the larva stage, and it is most interesting to collect these and breed them out. Wild collected larvae are nearly always subjected to a certain amount of parasitism, and you will soon see what an important part this plays in keeping down the numbers of butterflies in some years. In spite of this, many species of butterfly larvae are worth collecting and for some of them it is the only way you can obtain perfect specimens.

The Purple Hairstreak is one of these. It is hard to catch and is often damaged in the course of its buzzing zigzag flight, but you can 'beat' the larvae. The photograph shown on Plate 10 (below) was taken on the edge of a large wood. The sheet is attached to two long light poles to make it easier to handle. It can be placed flat on the ground or held by two persons if there are small bushes or growth under the trees. Choose an oak tree on the edge of a wood or in a large glade and tap the overhanging branches with a light pole as high up as you can reach. Many different larvae will come down, mostly moths and also a fine assortment of beetles and other insects. About the end of May you should find the larvae of the Purple Hairstreak which look rather like pale brown slugs $\frac{1}{2}$ in. (12 mm) long, with a black head which is tucked slightly under.

If you cannot get a friend and a large sheet you can use a small beating tray or even an upturned old umbrella. This will allow you to use only the lowest branches and the results will not be quite so good. You can also find the larvae of the White Letter Hairstreak in the same way, choosing a wych elm tree, preferably one standing by itself at the edge of a field, at a time when the bluebells are fully out. The larvae of the Brown Hairstreak can also be beaten with a

STUDYING INSECTS

small beating tray and you should seek a rather overgrown hedge of blackthorn along the edge of a field. Near the corners will be the best place, and if there are one or two small bushes actually in the corner, try these even if they are only a foot or two tall.

Probably the easiest caterpillars for a beginner to obtain are those from stinging-nettles. You can find the larvae of the Small Tortoiseshell which make quite a noticeable web on nettles. The larvae move off and make another web close by each time they change their skin, so be sure to look more carefully if you do not see them at first. In the last skin they all wander off and finally hang up to make their chrysalis. Peacock larvae can also be found in this way, but here you will need to examine clumps of nettle standing by themselves in a patch in a field.

Red Admirals also feed on nettle and you can find the larvae in August. These fold the leaf upwards along the main rib and then bite off the tip. Other larvae on nettle such as the Mother of Pearl moth don't make quite such a distinct fold and more often roll the leaf into a tube. You may find that a fair proportion of these various kinds will be 'stung' by parasites.

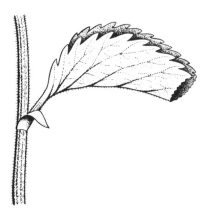

Fig. 25 Nettle leaf, folded and eaten by larva of the Red Admiral Butterfly

When breeding these larvae from nettle you must allow a clear space at the top of your cage, not brushed by food plant, and the larvae will all spin a little pad of silk and hang downwards to make their chrysalis. When they have all turned you should put a cylinder of brown paper round the cage to keep it dark. When they emerge the butterflies will sit quietly and not batter themselves to pieces.

So far I have not mentioned the 'White' caterpillars, which you can find on cabbage and related plants, including the nasturtium. The larvae are easy to find but are so heavily parasitized in some years that it is better to catch the butterflies on the wing, or obtain eggs from a female and breed a series. The Fritillary butterflies can sometimes be seen in small webs on their

BREEDING

food plant and you can find details of the plants, etc., in Appendix III at the end of this book and also in *The Observer's Book of Butterflies*. There is one exception to this method which will be mentioned on page 85.

The White Admiral butterfly is often chipped and torn when caught, for it loves bramble blossom and also flies in thick woodland. If you visit a wood in late May you can search for the larvae. The females of this butterfly like to lay their eggs in a fairly open wood, often one which has been coppiced and now has tall thin poles or trees spaced out. You may see thin wisps of honeysuckle climbing up and on these the eggs are laid. The larvae hibernate in a small twist of leaf which only the expert can find, but when they are bigger you can spot the feeding places and a freshly eaten leaf will 'bleed' and leave a bright raindrop of juice on the edge of the feeding place. If you look for this the larvae will not be far off. It is useless to examine huge clumps of honeysuckle outside woods.

The Purple Emperor, a close relative of the last species, is sometimes collected by finding eggs, but these later have to be hibernated as young larvae and it is a job for the more expert. You can beat fully grown larvae off sallow bushes, choosing a tree on the edge of a glade, half in and half out of the sun. I have found the larvae by searching the terminal twigs and buds just before the leaves open in the spring. The tiny larvae wake up from hibernation and walk up the twigs for food. They are quite conspicuous on the unopened buds but you need to recognize which bushes are the ones to examine or you will waste hours of time.

Many of the 'Brown' butterflies, including the Marbled White, Grayling, Meadow Brown, Gatekeeper, Speckled Wood and Wall, can be found by searching grass at night with a torch. The larvae will be there in the daytime but at night crawl farther up to feed and are more easily seen. The longer grass at the foot of downs or other hills is often one of the best places. The larvae are all very similar and you will probably get noctuid moth larvae at the same time. You will no doubt find many larvae of saw-flies feeding on grass, but these have more than three pairs of hind claspers and are slightly shiny in appearance, while the butterfly larvae have a rougher skin with a matt finish.

The larvae of the Skippers are too hard for the inexperienced to find; they mostly feed in a twist of grass but can more easily be obtained by catching the butterfly on the wing. The Small Copper can

STUDYING INSECTS

be found in the spring if you look on a clump of sorrel, especially on a bank. Search for oval holes in the leaves and the larvae will be concealed underneath.

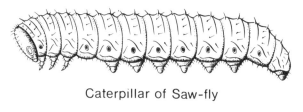

Caterpillar of Saw-fly

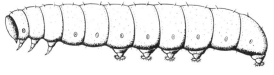

Caterpillar of Moth
Fig. 26

Most 'Blues' can be found easily. If you want larvae you must find the correct food plant and search it very carefully, choosing a place where you saw the butterflies flying the year before. Ants will 'milk' the larvae of most of the Blues for a sweet secretion; if you are looking at the plant you may suddenly see two or three ants rather more active than usual and close by you may see the larva.

The Holly Blue is an easier and more interesting species to find in the larva stage. You should find an old ivy-covered wall in a garden or park which is covered with ivy blossom just forming berries. The time is about September or slightly later. The larvae feed on or in the berries according to their size. When attacked, these berries produce a black stain like tar. Look for this and you will find a green slug-like larva. It will spend the winter as a chrysalis.

Moths

I have already mentioned one of the most profitable ways of finding caterpillars, the beating-tray method, and it is ideal for a great many species. I also mentioned searching at night for butterfly larvae. You can find moth larvae in this way also and you can sometimes obtain grass-feeding species by lying down flat and looking along the grass. Searching the bottoms of hedgerows and banks by night can be most entertaining, especially when the

BREEDING

Lappet moth larvae are fully grown and as large as cigars. Objects are inclined to look larger at night anyway and you can see these a long way off. Willow-herb is worth investigating at night for Hawks and so is yellow bedstraw, but you can find out from textbooks what food plants to examine and develop your own methods. In *The Observer's Book of Larger Moths* I have attempted to give the best way of getting results with each different species in the field, and if you follow the advice you will save yourself a lot of work.

You can 'sweep' for larvae with a kite-net frame, but using a linen bag instead of a netting one. This means walking up and down amongst low herbage and weaving your net amongst the plants so that larvae will be disturbed and fall in the net. It is an ideal way of finding the Beautiful Yellow Underwing on heather. To get the Cudweed Shark, a much rarer species, you have to be far more cunning. This feeds on golden-rod in clearings in large woods and the larvae spring off as you approach. If however you use two nets and, reaching out well in front of you, keep clapping them together over the plant, you should be successful.

Finding the larvae of microlepidoptera is fairly easy but more specialized and you must refer to L. T. Ford's *A Guide to the Smaller British Lepidoptera*, which will give you the plants and method of feeding. It generally means finding rolled leaves and flower heads, and examining leaves for mines and blisters and many other telltale signs of feeding. In the spring watch out for bent birch catkins. Pick these before they open out and they will contain the larvae of a micro; similarly, newly fallen cones of spruce, if they are bent, will also contain micro larvae. 'Bent' in both cases does not mean a gentle curve but a good kink.

A very easy and profitable way to find quite a number of microlepidoptera and also some beetles and other insects is to collect old birds' nests in the autumn. You should wait until the leaves are off the hedges and then collect a bagful of nests, choosing those with wool and hair or feathers inside. The nests of chaffinches and sparrows are two suitable kinds. Tits' nests from nesting-boxes will have a few species but there are many others you can try. These nests can be kept in a deep wooden box during the winter. See that the top is quite level and then all you need is a sheet of glass over them. It will be necessary to sprinkle water on the nests when emergences are expected in the spring. You can expect several interesting species by this method, including the common clothes moth!

STUDYING INSECTS
THE CATERPILLAR STAGE
Cages
Caterpillars are reared either in some form of cage or enclosed in a muslin tube on their natural food plant. When using a cage the whole food plant, growing in a pot, may be used or if the plant is too big, shoots of it are supplied regularly and kept fresh in a vessel in water.

A cage which will give you moderate results can be made in a great number of ways, but the cage which will give the maximum results for the greatest number of species is the cylinder type (Fig. 27). These are not easy for an amateur to make but they are cheap to buy. The better type of cage has a high-impact polystyrene base and lid, the lid having a circle of gauze in it, and a semi-rigid, clear plastic cylinder. Properly used they are ideal. You can misuse them by placing them in hot sun when housing larvae and by filling them with far too much food. This will become stale before it is consumed, and generally all overcrowding is bad. Hot sun will cause rapid condensation on the sides of the cage. This is undesirable since larvae walking on the sides might drown, the food will have moisture extracted from it, which will toughen it and cause constipation, and lastly it will encourage mould.

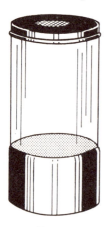

Fig. 27
Cylinder breeding cage

The great advantage of these cages is that you can disinfect them once a year with hot water to which a disinfectant has been added. The various parts are interchangeable and they separate at the base as well as at the lid. This means that if you have a number of butterfly pupae hanging down from the lid which do not want to be disturbed you can change this lid for another fresh one. The base of the cage can also be used to contain earth, and this will serve to hold your food jar steady if it is pushed a little way down.

The earlier type of wooden cage with a sliding glass front is dangerous. You need only have a caterpillar or, what is even worse, a chrysalis on the glass and you cannot withdraw the glass and there is no other door.

If you are on holiday and haven't a cage, you can use a large paper bag. Place the food plant in, head first, with your larvae and then tie a piece of string tightly round the bag and stems and stand it in a jar of water. You cannot watch the progress of the larvae but by holding the bag against the light you can tell if more food is required. The cylinder type of cage can be taken on holiday since the top part will close on the lower with the larvae safely inside, and then the whole of this will slide into the middle of the plastic cylinder for packing.

Although I would not generally recommend wooden cages because they harbour germs, it is possible to make a temporary wooden cage out of a box. The total cost of this is so low that you can burn it as soon as you see any signs of disease. You require a wooden box which is nearly twice as long as it is high. It need not be square at the ends but the longer the better, since this gives you height for food plants, and it need not have a lid.

Stand the box on end, remove the boards from the back, as in Fig. 28(2), and make sure the sides are securely nailed. Then proceed as instructed in Fig. 28. This type of do-it-yourself cage will last longer if you pin up on the roof inside a piece of strong brown paper, cut to fit, and also line the bottom with two layers of newspaper. This helps to trap the surplus fluid (see top of page 131) which butterflies can 'spill' when they hatch out. This fluid can be very infectious, as Pasteur discovered when he did research on silk-worms. All the paper can be burnt when emergences are finished. The chief advantage of this easily made cage is that it allows height and room for food plants in jars. Always stand your home-made cage with the back to the light so that when you open the door nothing will fly out and larvae will not be in the way of shutting the door.

Polythene bags, although good for certain types of collecting, are not recommended for breeding. They are too air-tight and this leads to condensation, which means the plants of food material lose moisture; this leads to a slight wilting or toughening of the leaves which in turn will block the intestinal canal of the larva and take too long to pass through. This will give bacteria time to multiply and soon the larvae turn flaccid and die. This also applies to other forms of the same material such as boxes and sandwich boxes. These boxes work very well for some species but should be cleaned every day and fresh food added.

Sleeving larvae

Today there are various types of horticultural plastic germinators. Some of these have a small heating unit or light bulb under them

STUDYING INSECTS

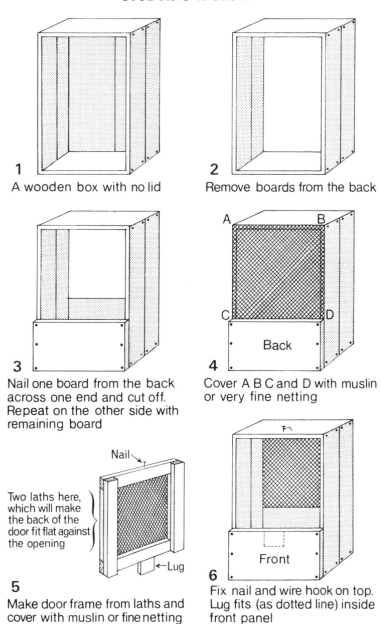

1 A wooden box with no lid

2 Remove boards from the back

3 Nail one board from the back across one end and cut off. Repeat on the other side with remaining board

4 Cover A B C and D with muslin or very fine netting

5 Make door frame from laths and cover with muslin or fine netting

6 Fix nail and wire hook on top. Lug fits (as dotted line) inside front panel

Fig. 28 Do-it-yourself cage

BREEDING

and are quite suitable for forcing pupae, especially if you maintain the humidity. They are, however, unsuitable for rearing larvae, for they are too low and do not allow enough room for food. You can have growing food such as violets, on which various Fritillaries will feed, but condensation will occur, and, as mentioned earlier, larvae will drown in it, for they wander off the food to fasten themselves on the sides while they perform a change of skin.

If there is the slightest trace of the flaccid disease in any larvae it spreads very quickly under damp, humid and airless conditions, and you will have great difficulty in eradicating it. It is safer to forgo the joy of seeing things through transparent plastic and to use a sleeve on a pot of growing food plant.

Sleeving is one of the more natural ways to rear larvae of any type. This can be done on a branch or on a plant or even on a cabbage. A sleeve consists of a muslin tube with open ends. You slip it along a branch and tie the lower end. Place in your larvae and tie the top end. Again, do not put in too much food and tie the ends carefully or you will make a happy home for earwigs which will soon eat your larvae (Plate 10, above).

Muslin is a rather loose term. You require a material which will be fairly airy but not too open. Cheese cloth is too flimsy but a material such as unbleached calico, with the weave not too dense, would be a good choice. There are various types of nylon available, but although these are strong they are often too transparent. If the birds can see larvae through the sleeving material they will attack the sleeve. The material needs to be dense enough to conceal the larvae completely, yet at the same time let in air. Tiffany is the ideal material, but although large quantities are imported annually from India, it is not found in every fabric shop. Sometimes shops which handle theatrical materials stock it, as it can be used for stretching across wooden frames and painted for scenery.

Be careful when using sleeves to change them on to a fresh branch just before the food becomes exhausted. If you leave it too late the larvae will wander on to the sides of the sleeves and will get attacked by tits, who will not only damage your larvae but will make holes all over the sleeve. With species which require earth or peat for burying in while they pupate, such as Lime Hawks – a good species to sleeve since lime-tree cuttings soon wilt in water – you should choose a branch with one end much higher than the other.

You can pack the lower end with moss when the larvae get into

STUDYING INSECTS

their last skin and if you open this end every day or so, you can remove those larvae among the moss and place them in a cage for pupation. When ready for pupation these larvae will turn dark brown in colour. If you adopt this method, be sure to wrap a piece of sacking round the lower end of the sleeve to keep the tits away.

The care of young caterpillars

The first critical stage for larvae is when they come out of their eggs. They are very small at this stage and also very delicate, so you should handle them with care. Moving them from old leaves to fresh leaves can be assisted by gently lifting them with a fine camel's-hair brush.

Larvae will change their skins four or five times and you must take this into consideration as it is most important. To achieve these skin changes, the larvae will first fasten themselves on to a leaf or twig with a small silk pad. This is not always easily visible and you must take care not to move these larvae. The purpose of the silk pad is to anchor the old skin. You will see the larval head start to grow, the old 'head piece' appearing to go downwards as the new head grows inside. The old head will then drop off, the skin split and the larva walk forwards and out. It will be delicate and soft at first. If you move one during this change it cannot escape from its skin, which sometimes gets into a tight girdle and kills the larva.

When using jars of food plant in water be sure to pack the neck of the jar in such a way that larvae cannot crawl down the jar into the water and drown themselves. The Large Elephant Hawk larvae have a passion for getting into water. It is often the best plan to use little food and two jars. A fresh one can be placed alongside the old one and the larvae can then walk across. This avoids handling.

Apart from the risk to the larvae of undue handling, some larvae cannot be handled without slight risk to yourself. Amongst the worst of these are perhaps the larvae of the Oak Eggar and the Fox moth. These larvae have firm long hairs which will stick into the softer parts of the skin, generally between the fingers, and this may cause a slight rash or urtication. The worst offender in this respect is the Browntail moth larva, as this feeds in a web and the hairs become loose naturally and are likely to fly about in a wind and get down your neck. This species should be handled with extreme caution, while other larvae only require common sense and reasonable care.

BREEDING
Rearing silk-worms
When silk-worms are bred on a commercial basis they are fed for so many days, starved for so many days when skin changing takes place, then fed again for so many days, and so on. Everything is worked out by calendar and any larvae which fall behind are discarded as being disease-prone or from poor stock.

Although the silk-worm is a cultured foreign species, those who use this book for educational purposes may like to have a few simple rules on the method of keeping it. The eggs of the silk-worm pass the winter in this stage when they are imported, generally from Italy. Although you can keep quite good strains going from year to year, it is better to obtain a good fresh stock when possible since these will be very much stronger and produce far better cocoons.

Commercial breeders store their 'seed' or eggs in controlled incubators. This retards the eggs until the leaves are ready on the bushes, since you do not want to strip the early shoots and damage the bushes when a week or two later you can have food in abundance. This point should be remembered by the amateur, so don't keep your eggs in a warm room but retard them as long as possible. They will keep well in the bottom of an ordinary household refrigerator.

The best food, if you can obtain it, is undoubtedly the leaves of the mulberry, and in the early stages when the larvae or 'worms' are young, the food should be cut into strips with scissors to provide more leaf edges from which the larvae start eating. If you cannot obtain mulberry leaves, very slightly wilted lettuce will do as a substitute, but the results are nothing like so good. You can switch from lettuce to mulberry leaves, but the larvae will not take to lettuce after being started on mulberry. Many schools now plant a mulberry bush in a suitable corner, and these trees will keep alive for centuries. Some of them in old country gardens were planted in the reign of Charles I and are still standing.

You do not require a cage for breeding silk-worms, a lid from a shoe-box being all that is necessary. The insects have been pampered for so many thousands of generations that they have lost the power to wander about or climb trees. You could not, for instance, sleeve them on the growing bush. Don't leave your box lid on the floor where mice might help themselves, and don't leave it by an open window where tits or a tame robin might find them. They also perish if left in a draught.

STUDYING INSECTS

The worms will make several skin changes before becoming fully grown; when they reach this stage the first sign to watch for is a larva which has found its way into a corner and has started to weave its head about as if looking for something. Larvae in this condition should be removed and each one placed separately in a paper cone, with the top tucked in. This will ensure a confined space for cocoon weaving, the object being to provide a scaffolding for the construction. If you don't do this the larva will wander about trying various places and wasting a lot of its silk needlessly.

When the cocoon is completed the larva will pupate. About ten days after it has started, gently shake the paper cone and if it rattles there is a sound pupa inside. If you want to keep the silk you must remove it at once; if you leave it, the moth will emerge and in so doing will spit a special fluid on the silk and force its way out, cutting most of the strands so that unwinding is impossible.

To save some of your own silk, remove all the outer loose silk from the cocoon and then soak the firm cocoon in warm water. If you gently finger it and pull at the sides, a strand or two of silk will come away. Keep pulling this out until you are left with a single strand which will be a continuous thread.

There is little the amateur can do with his own silk. Commercially, several cocoons are unwound together and twisted up at the same time into one continuous, thicker strand which is then made into skeins for the weavers. You can wind your silk off on a postcard lengthways in three different places. Then cut across the three rings you have made and plait them into a book-marker.

The last portion of the cocoon will have to be left since it is difficult to unwind and often of a weak thread. The pupa will still be alive, unless your water was too hot, and this can be placed on a tray covered with clean paper. The moths will emerge quite quickly and will pair at once. After a day or two it is advisable to remove many of the males so that the females can lay all their eggs without interference. The eggs will be pale yellow and if fertile will soon turn dark grey. You can then cut the patches off the paper and store in a clean tin. The silk-worm is single-brooded so these will keep until the next season. There are certain bi-voltine strains, but these are not in general circulation. You can spread out your own stocks by retarding some in the refrigerator. This makes them suitable for school use, as you can adjust the timing to suit the school term.

BREEDING
THE CHRYSALIS STAGE

Pupation

Pupation requires a little care, for the larvae will cast off their old and last skin and reveal the chrysalis. This will be pale and soft at first but will soon harden and darken; if while still soft it is crowded into a small space or up against a stone, it will harden out of shape and you will ultimately get a crippled moth.

Many species like to wriggle down into the ground and you should cater for this by placing in the bottom of your cage some bulb fibre, peat, soft mould or even sand. The Privet Hawk moth likes to burrow much deeper than other species, and you should not have too many in a small space or they may cripple one another by overcrowding. The Large Elephant Hawk larvae like moss on top of the soil and they burrow under this, make a shallow scoop in the soil, and then pupate.

Other species require old plant stems with a nice pith centre into which they can enter. The well-known microlepidopterist S. N. A. Jacobs used to pin 3-in. (8-cm) strips of corrugated paper right round certain warehouse walls, and grain and other moth pests would use the small tubes in this paper for their cocoons. He could then take it down and give his grateful friends a yard of mixed pupae which was very well received!

I have adopted this idea many times when breeding larvae in various types of blossom. These are apt to mould rapidly especially when in bulk in a confined space, but strips of corrugated paper collected most of the pupae which could then be removed to a safer place.

A method of keeping down mould is to sprinkle with a 2 per cent solution of common salt (Fig. 29). This is safe even to put on leaves which larvae may eat and it helps a great deal where you have food in a jar standing in peat in which larvae are pupating. You will have a fair amount of larval excrement on the bottom of the cage and it is not safe to disturb this until all the larvae have finished burrowing down. The salt solution will help to reduce mould on this. It is also useful to combat the fungus which attacks Fox moth larvae. These larvae can be found fully grown sitting in the sun on hilly grasslands in the autumn. They make a slight scoop in the ground under moss or loose turf but do not pupate until the spring. During the winter a rather high proportion die from a white fungus or mould. Autumn-collected Fox moth larvae can be put in a

STUDYING INSECTS

refrigerator for about three weeks, then gradually warmed up, and they will emerge before Christmas.

Goat moth larvae require rotten wood for their pupation. They make a cocoon in this in the autumn which is really a hibernaculum in which they pass the winter. In the spring they come out and make a proper cocoon in which they finally pupate.

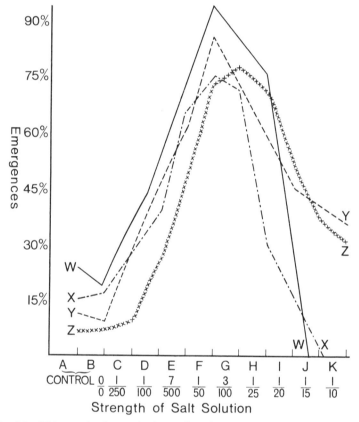

Fig. 29 This graph shows the immediate increase in successful emergences when salt solution is used. There is a rapid decrease in emergences when the solution becomes too strong. *Reproduced by permission of the Royal Entomological Society; from an original paper by R. L. E. Ford.*

Storing pupae

Overwintering butterfly pupae such as the 'Whites' may often be left quite safely on the sides or roof of the cage where they have

BREEDING

spun their pad and girdle of silk. In fact it is not good to disturb them and the effect is the same as disturbing larvae which are changing their skins; they cannot walk out of the empty chrysalis unless it is attached to something.

However, if moth pupae are in peat or soil of some sort they should be dug up and stored in clean tins. You must of course wait until they are hard enough to handle before you disturb them. The tins are best stored in a cold dry place; cold will not harm them but mould and damp will.

Emergence

The pupae of the Hawk moths overwinter very well, but you should not put them into permanent store until mid-September, as there may be a partial emergence of a second brood. This happens more often with Poplar Hawks than with other species, especially if you had an early brood in the first instance. If you breed the interesting hybrid between the Poplar and the Eyed Hawk, you must watch the pupae most carefully, as these will often emerge as late as the beginning of October.

In the spring you may place your pupae in a cage on a layer of moss and you may also lay a very thin layer of moss on top. The variety of moss is the fine feathery type and not the solid type which has to be dug up on a block of earth.

When emergence is due, the moss should be kept damp with water. You should also place suitable twigs near by on to which your specimens can climb. They will then hang down to allow their wings to expand fully and then dry. Both moths and butterflies do this. Once a moth has dried its wings, it will move them from what might be termed the butterfly position to the one they normally adopt when at rest. You must never kill immature specimens since they are limp and cannot be set.

Sexing pupae

It is possible in many species to tell the sex of pupae. (Fig. 30 shows how this may be done by examining the underside of the tip.) The advantage of this is great when you are breeding certain species, particularly the Large Elephant Hawk. The sex of this species is not easy to tell in the adult. The bodies all look fat and the claspers at the tip of the tail, which may be seen in many other males, are hidden by fluff. You may therefore put into a cage two males or two females hoping for eggs, and you will get only damaged and worn specimens. If you can separate your sexes into two different cages you can take one from each and are certain of obtaining eggs.

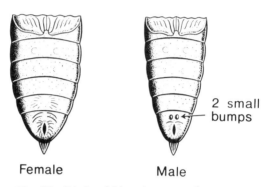

Fig. 30 Distinguishing the sexes of pupae

In most species of moths and butterflies males nearly always emerge a day or two before the females. This is a provision of nature to ensure that when a female is out there will be males ready for mating. In this country the sexes are generally about even in numbers but in the tropics there are many more males than females.

Pupa digging

This is a good winter pastime if you don't choose a day with a freezing cold wind blowing. The idea is to loosen the soil round the base of certain trees and find pupae (Plate 11, right). It only works well if you acquire an eye for a likely tree, one which stands a little by itself and has tufts of grass round the base. This grass can be turned back and pupae will often be just underneath, or you may have to loosen a little soil round the roots. Trees which have closely packed bare earth round them are not very profitable and trees which have had cattle tramping round their base are also best left alone, for the pupae are generally crippled. Experience will tell you the best trees to select but poplars are best for Poplar and Eyed Hawk moths. (The former will have a rough pupa and the latter a smooth one.) Lime trees and large oaks are also worth trying.

BREEDING

Forcing pupae

The emergence time of pupae may be altered by collectors for their own convenience. Many species of moth pass the winter in the pupa stage and you can force these to emerge some months earlier so that you can set them at your leisure and not at the height of the busy season. If you do this you may not be able to breed a further series from your stock since food plants will not always be available out of season, and pairing and egg laying under artificial conditions will also present difficulties. You will not be able to assemble any wild males, but if you have a number of pupae and only require to set a series, forcing is to be recommended.

To force pupae you need a cylinder-type breeding cage with a few inches of sand on the bottom. Cover this with moss as described under 'Emergence' on page 77 and place on top of a stove such as a kitchen boiler if this is of a type which is slow burning and does not get too hot. Anthracite stoves are suitable and so is the hot tank in the linen cupboard if you are allowed to use this. You must remember that heat will dry things out and your moss must be dampened each day. Pupae force very quickly under these conditions.

The pupae of the Death's Head moth require special care. Although these pupate in the autumn like other hawks, they do not overwinter like other species but are continuous brooded and will wish to emerge after a fairly short period. This is generally prevented by the onset of cold weather and you must always force them in the following manner. Use a deep flower-pot with sand and moss as before, but stand the pot in a saucer of water as well as dampening the moss; a linen cupboard is generally warm enough without having to stand the container actually on a tank. Your pot is covered with muslin and you should see that there is enough room for the wings to develop since these will be much longer than usual, the Death's Head being the largest of the Hawk moths. The total time taken is about three to four weeks, or six weeks after the larvae first burrowed to pupate.

FURTHER BREEDING METHODS

Microlepidoptera

Now that more literature is available on the smaller moths (*British Pyralid and Plume Moths* by Bryan P. Beirne-Warne covers one whole large group), more collectors are turning their attention to these and finding their study and their biology extremely fascinating subjects. These moths include the Pyrales, a very large group containing a number of quite large moths; the Plume moths, a very small distinct group having wings like feathers; and the Tortrices, another large group containing some very colourful species. The remainder of the smaller moths are often lumped into one very large group called the tineids. They are generally too small for the beginner but should certainly be studied at some time, for under a lens some of these are the most beautiful of all. They include the case-carrying caterpillars, which live in a case that they make for concealment, the leaf miners and many others. The life history and food plants of the microlepidoptera, which form a guide to their collection and study, are very well covered by *A Guide to the Smaller British Lepidoptera* by L. T. Ford.

The microlepidoptera are not really different from other moths, except that they are mostly smaller, the term being one of convenience. They are more easily collected by looking for the larvae, or rather the feeding places of the larvae, which are almost all concealed in some manner. The outward signs of their feeding betray them to the initiated. You look for leaf mines, rolled or folded leaves, galls, blisters in or under leaves, wilted shoots and many other indications. These are all described in the book mentioned at the end of the preceding paragraph.

Their method of rearing is, however, worth mentioning here since it can also be used for many other insects. You can breed saw-flies, gall-making flies and some beetles by the same method, and the most important factor is moisture control. If too much moisture is present small larvae may even drown. Capillary attraction takes water into the small tubes they make of silk or in spun leaves or borings in shoots and cuts off the air supply.

The ideal way of keeping many species of larvae which use spun leaves or mine in leaves is to gather them when they are nearly fully grown and keep them in a flower-pot or earthenware seed pan. In these days of plastics I had better stipulate an earthenware flower-pot as this is half the secret of success. You first select a sound pot with a fairly level top and about 8 in. (20 cm) across. You next require a perfectly flat surface of stone or cement or an artificial paving slab. Next turn your pot upside-down on the slab and pour water on the slab. If you hold the pot firmly with both hands and move your hands round in a circle you will grind the top rim of the pot quite flat. This does not take long. The pot should then be half filled with clean fresh sand and the top covered with a square of plate glass. This should be quite evenly flat and thus makes a perfectly tight join that even the smallest of larvae cannot worm their way through.

The occupied leaves, etc., are placed on the sand in an even layer and the pot is then stood on a shelf well below eye level in the shade in a place of fairly even temperature. If the sun gets to it the leaves dry up too quickly. You will notice at first that many beads of moisture will condense on the underside of the plate glass. In the mornings you therefore turn the glass over and allow it to dry off. You might think it necessary to repeat this process in the evenings as well. After a day or two this will probably stop and you will have a few days with an almost dry glass.

If your larvae are still feeding you should keep things moist, so lift the glass and sprinkle a few drops of water. If this is too much you will again see the condensation on the glass and you will soon learn to control the amount of humidity to within very fine limits. If your larvae are pupating, however, you can let everything become quite dry and only add moisture again just as emergence is commencing; very little is required. If parasites are being reared from cocoons, the slight humidity at this stage makes all the difference between hatching out just a few and one hundred per cent successful emergence. Too much moisture won't stop the emergence but small moths would get caught in the beads of condensation on the glass.

I once made some plate-glass circles for the flower-pot tops. This is a great mistake as the square ones are much more useful. When insects emerge they sit on the glass. If there are a lot it might be safer to lift the glass in front of a closed window where there is a strong light outside. The insects will then fly on to the window and can be examined and boxed.

If, however, only one or two specimens have emerged and they are sitting on the underside of the glass cover, it is quicker to remove the lid from a glass-bottomed pill-box and put the box under one of the corners of the glass sheet which covers the pot. Gently lift up the glass sheet, move the pill-box under the insect and it will fall into the bottom of your box. Before it flies up to the glass again, quickly slide the box across to a corner of the glass sheet and lower the glass. If the insect then jumps up to sit on the glass sheet, a slight tap on the glass or a movement of your pill-box

STUDYING INSECTS

will make it drop in again and you can put the box lid back on. This operation is not possible if you use a circular glass sheet to cover your pot.

It is quite safe to overwinter your pupae or pre-pupae in these pots or seed pans providing you have them dry and on a shelf under cover. Pre-pupae are larvae which are fully developed and ready to pupate but which pass long periods, such as the whole of the winter months, in this state and only pupate a short time before

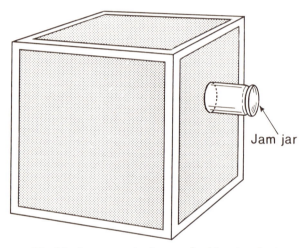

Fig. 31 Large wooden box, preferably a tea chest, in which plant material can be kept

the adult moth emerges, so that the pupal stage proper is only the same length as that of a quick summer-brooded species. One species of micro feeds on sea lavender and passes from September until the end of the following July inside the plant stem as a pre-pupa.

If you have plant stems of this woody nature – and there are many stems worth gathering in the autumn: thistle, burdock and teasel for example – these can be overwintered in a muslin bag and hung out of doors. Don't push a bunch in a bag, tie the top and then hang it by the string. This would leave all the stems upside-down; moisture would run down inside the cut stems and since there is no escape at the other end the insects might drown or get mouldy. It is better to store the stems the correct way up; I generally hang mine where they will get a little natural rain but are sheltered from a real downpour.

BREEDING

If at any time you are engaged on research which involves the keeping of a great quantity of plant material over the winter from which you hope various insects will emerge in the spring, the following apparatus will help you. You need a large wooden box such as an empty tea chest with a sound lid, a large size jam jar and a glass cutter. Place the glass cutter on a match-box with the wheel or diamond against the side of the upright jam jar. Rotate the jar so that you cut it slightly all round at an even height. If you then heat a poker red-hot and align it on your cutting mark you will hear a loud click and a crack will run round the jar where you have marked it. It may not go right round at first but after the second attempt all you need is a slight tap and the bottom of the jam jar will drop off leaving a neat cut.

You then place your jar against the side of the tea chest about three-quarters of the way up and mark a circle. It is a little harder to cut this circle out neatly; an extremely sharp-pointed knife is my favourite tool for the job. The jam jar should now make a snug fit into the hole and it should be pushed in only about 1 in. (2 cm), leaving the top end outside. The reason for this is that you can cover it with muslin held in place with an elastic band, or thin string if you leave it all the winter.

Your plant material, if it is fairly dry, can now be placed inside and the lid secured. The chest must of course be kept under cover and you can watch for emergences. Any insect will go towards the light and enter the jar where you can see it. You may get a few spiders to start with which must of course be removed. During the time that insects may be expected to emerge you must sprinkle with water as before.

Insects which do well in this type of contrivance are Plume moths in the stems of *Eupatorium* and the case-bearing *Coleophora*, or *Eupista* as it is now called. Some species of this last group feed among the seed heads of plants such as wild golden-rod and it is quicker to collect a large bunch of the stems when the seed is about ripe than attempt to search for individual larval cases.

Plant tubs

If you wish to keep insects on growing plants the best way is to have the plant in a good-sized flower-pot or wooden tub. A garden cane is stuck in the centre and then a muslin tube or sleeve is placed so that one end is over the rim of the container and the other

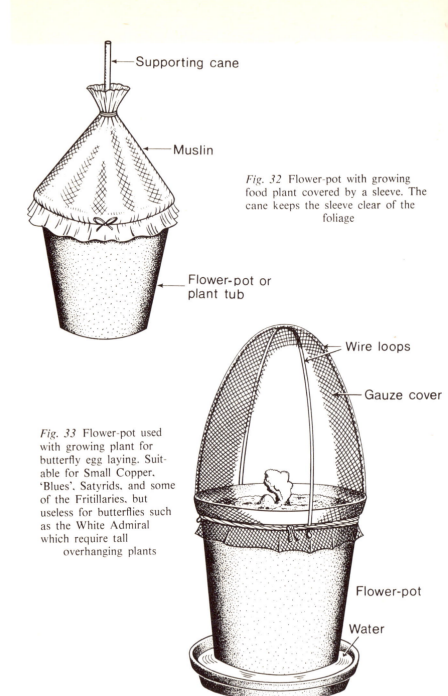

Fig. 32 Flower-pot with growing food plant covered by a sleeve. The cane keeps the sleeve clear of the foliage

Fig. 33 Flower-pot used with growing plant for butterfly egg laying. Suitable for Small Copper, 'Blues', Satyrids, and some of the Fritillaries, but useless for butterflies such as the White Admiral which require tall overhanging plants

BREEDING

is tied round the top of the cane. The golden rule is never to try to keep things in a square box since you can never tie a string tightly round it; it is only caterpillar proof at the four corners. A lightweight wooden frame will hold muslin round the edge of a box if you have nothing else to hand. You must be very careful when using planted material not to include slugs, spiders, earwigs, woodlice or any insects other than the ones you wish to rear.

In some cases such as the Marsh or Greasy Fritillary you can plant scabious in a flower-pot and make a wire frame over the top with enough space for a small jar of suitable flowers on which the butterflies can feed. Your butterflies will lay on the scabious leaves and later the small larvae will hibernate all together in a little web. You can then take them off the wire cage and use a muslin sleeve for the winter.

Preserving Larvae

The most popular way of preserving larvae of Lepidoptera for educational use is by 'blowing'. This consists of removing the contents of the larva and then inflating it like a balloon and drying it hard while in this position. This method is of no use for preserving larvae for purely scientific purposes since besides damaging certain parts it does not keep the insides; larvae required for scientific work are best preserved in fluids as described on page 91.

Larvae 'blowing'

To preserve a larva by the blowing method you must of course first kill your specimen. If a larva dies naturally you can use this if you do not keep it too long. If it has died from a flaccid disease it will be no good, for the skin will have perished. If it has been parasitized by the braconid family, *Apanteles*, it will also be quite useless as it will be perforated all over! You will therefore probably have to kill a sound specimen unless perhaps you have one which has crawled into the food-plant jar and drowned itself.

Place your dead larva on a sheet of blotting-paper with the head towards you and cover it with a second sheet which may be much smaller. Press the larva slightly from the head end. Next take a needle, such as a setting needle, in a handle and either assist the skin at the anal end to turn slightly inside out or actually pierce a hole at this point. You will have to raise the top sheet of blotting-paper to see what you are doing, so take care not to get a squirt in your eyes. Too sudden or great a pressure will burst your specimen, so proceed slowly. The body contents can be gently squeezed out and once this has begun you can assist a little with the needle or with fine forceps. Some books refer to 'rolling out' the contents. This really means a gentle pressure with something like a pencil which is rolled from the head towards the larva tail. It does

PRESERVING LARVAE

not mean putting the specimen through a mangle. If too much force is used you will destroy the colouring and markings which are stored between the outer and inner skins of the larva and should be left untouched. Too much pressure will remove the inner skin and leave you with a thin transparent tube.

I advise the beginner to choose an easy larva such as that of the Large White butterfly. This is not hairy and it also keeps its colour and markings very well. The Small White larva, which is plain green, will lose all its colour and will have to be treated as described on page 90.

Hairy larvae are much harder and should be left until you are more skilled at the work. The larva of the Garden Tiger or 'woolly bear' has very long hairs which come out easily and nothing looks worse than a bald specimen.

This difficulty can be overcome by two methods which help a great deal. Firstly, choose your larvae carefully; one which is about to make its chrysalis will be inclined to lose its hairs very easily. The Garden Tiger spins an outer web for its cocoon and all its hairs drop out and are incorporated in the web. It is best to select a specimen which has changed to the last skin about two days earlier. Secondly, you can extract the body contents by holding the larva very gently between the finger and thumb making sure that the hairs all lie one way. Gentle pressure and assistance with forceps are essential. The contents are pulled rather than squeezed out and you should never use a roller.

The next stage in blowing is to mount your larvae on a suitable glass tube. Heat a tube and draw it out, which will leave you with two pieces each with very fine points. Cut these with a file at different places so that you have different sized tubes for different larvae. Obviously you will want a fine tube for a small specimen. (Fig. 34.)

The tube is completed by adding a small piece of watch-spring held on by wire or a small rubber band made by cutting a thin slice off a rubber tube. You will require a length of rubber tube on the glass to connect with your mouth. The point of the tube is next inserted into the anal end of the larva. If the opening is hard to see because the skin is very thin or squashed flat, try to find a drop more moisture to squeeze out, or even retain a small drop especially for this purpose. Just as this drop is extruded the skin will open and at the right moment you can slide the glass tube in. The larva is held on the glass tube by the spring clip – it does not matter which way up; you will learn it varies with the species being treated. Often the anal flap at the top of the larva will make a convenient place for the clip to get a good grip. If you use the underside, however, be careful not to knock off the last pair of larval claspers when you attempt to get the specimen off the glass tube.

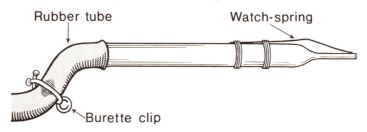

Fig. 34 Larva-blowing tube of drawn glass

Having got your specimen on the tube, gently inflate it and you will find it will extend to normal size. Don't use too much force and stretch it beyond its natural size. With luck it will remain air-tight, but if air escapes through the mouth or elsewhere you will have to keep on blowing all the time.

You now require a hot-air oven which may be made from a small tin mounted on wire legs (Fig. 35). A spirit lamp is placed under the oven and the mounted larva held inside. Drying does not take long. It is advisable to get the tube well in so that the tail dries first and you can slowly withdraw it to finish the head end. If the head is dried first, you may burn the specimen while you are finishing the tail end.

Fig. 35 Larva-blowing oven

PRESERVING LARVAE

From time to time you can test the progress by taking out the tube from the oven and gently pressing the head towards the tail. If it is quite dry you will find the whole skin quite rigid. If not ready it will sag or dent where it is still soft and will need longer in the oven. You can turn it over to the place required but at this stage watch for burning. It is better to do long-haired larvae more slowly in an oven which is not nearly so hot. This may take longer and so your jaws will ache with blowing. You can avoid this by buying a double rubber bellows which is worked by hand and which keeps a constant pressure since one of the rubber 'bags' acts as a reservoir for the air.

Having dried your larva to the correct degree, you can remove it from the glass tube by lifting the spring and seeing if you can gently prise it off. It may stick, particularly under the part where the spring touched. If it will not come off, you can touch the tube with a tiny bead of vaseline on a pin. The tube will still be hot and the vaseline will run under the end of the larva which can then be removed. The snag to watch for here is not to use too much vaseline or your specimen will become greasy.

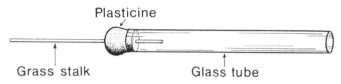

Fig. 36 Grass stalk used as a larva-blowing tube

When blowing very tiny larvae of the microlepidoptera, I often use a grass stalk instead of a fine glass tube (Fig. 36). Find a fine dried stalk and fix it in the end of a glass tube with a small amount of plasticine. No clip is required to retain the larva on the grass stalk, and only very slight air pressure should be used to inflate the larva. When the larva has dried, which will only take about a minute, cut the stalk carefully, allowing sufficient for pinning, and use the end for the next one. (For further techniques, see page 91.)

Mounting

There are many ways in which you can mount blown larvae but the most popular is to get some green-covered copper wire, glue the larvae on one end of this (Fig. 37), and wind the other end round a pin. The same pin also carries the data label.

STUDYING INSECTS

The micro larvae on grass stalks are a little more difficult. You can put a pin through the end of the stalk. The stalk will almost certainly split and you must add some glue. Alternatively, you can cut the grass stalk close to the end of the larva and mount on wire, or you can insert the end of the grass stalk into a small piece of polyporus and then put a pin through the polyporus. Some collectors prefer to mount on natural twigs but they can take up a great deal of valuable cabinet space.

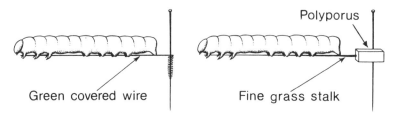

Fig. 37 Two methods of mounting blown larvae

Colouring

The colouring of green and other larvae is difficult. There are several ways of doing this. Small thin-skinned larvae may be coloured by taking fine-quality artist's pastels or crayons (chalk and not wax) and grinding them to very fine powder. A little of this can be tipped into the hole in the end of the larva with a paper chute and the specimen is then gently shaken to distribute the powder evenly. Any surplus is tipped out and if you have used the correct colouring, the specimen should look extremely lifelike since it is coloured from the inside. I once made for myself a little puffer for powdered chalk. It tipped the powder in at the large opening and this was then closed with a finger or a small cork. The puff is provided by the normal rubber teat from a pipette (Fig. 38).

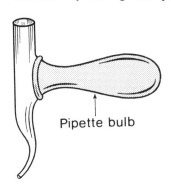

Fig. 38 Pipette for inserting coloured chalk into blown larvae

PRESERVING LARVAE

Another method is to use stains. These have to be soluble in spirit and not water or you will soften the skin of the specimen which will then go out of shape. A better method is to paint them by hand but do not use too much paint. Some larvae appear to have oily surfaces and when you use water paints these run into beads. The old remedy was ox-gall bought from an art shop but today a little of any of the modern detergents added to your paint will stop it 'beading' and make the task of colouring extremely interesting.

The 'freeze-drying' technique

There has recently been developed an entirely new preservation technique – the 'freeze drying' process – but unfortunately it is not one easily used by an amateur.

When a caterpillar dies, the muscles become inactive and the body goes limp. This is due to the atmospheric pressure acting on the skin outside. If you place a dead larva in a vacuum, then it will retain its shape. If you have moist objects in a refrigerator the water is partly extracted, and the object is then dehydrated. The new process combines these two principles so that an object in a vacuum has its water content removed by freezing. The result is that the object is dried out and there being no atmospheric pressure while this is happening, it retains its natural shape. Of course, the body contents remain in caterpillars, and if you use this method it will make them slightly more attractive to the museum beetle and mites; but this point is a small risk. It is more serious with birds and animals since they are subject to more and larger insect pests when dried in this way.

At the moment, the apparatus required is rather large and expensive, and only a fortunate few can have access to this method. However, it is still early days, and in time it is hoped something more compact can be manufactured as I think it has very great and interesting possibilities.

Storing larvae in fluid

Larvae can be preserved in fluid quite easily using ethyl alcohol, about 75 to 80 per cent. The beginner can use ordinary methylated spirit which works quite well but is coloured. This colour generally disappears with use but you can sometimes remove it by filtering through granulated charcoal.

STUDYING INSECTS

Spirits of wine as sold by a chemist is pure or absolute alcohol and this is very expensive. Commercial alcohol is similar to uncoloured methylated spirit but is obtainable only if you get a licence from your local Excise office, and unless you require a great quantity this is not worth all the trouble. Quite a popular fluid is Pampel's mixture, which consists of glacial acetic acid 4 c.c., distilled water 30 c.c., formaldehyde (40 per cent) 6 c.c., alcohol (95 per cent) 15 c.c.

The larvae to be preserved are kept in small tubes. It is most essential when preserving anything in fluid to prevent the subject from swishing about, for it will soon get damaged and come apart. This means placing a little cotton wool in the tube before adding the specimen and placing a little more on top afterwards. A data label (pencil or Indian ink only) can be slipped down the side. Storage presents a problem. It is not possible to cork small tubes efficiently so it is better to immerse all the tubes in your fluid in a larger jar with a ground-glass stopper.

Some workers put little numbers upside-down in the bottom of tubes and then keep the tubes upside-down in the jar. You can keep an index of the contents with a guide to the numbers; but whatever you do, don't take a short cut and leave out your data from each tube, simply placing this in a notebook with a number against it. If the book is lost the whole collection is quite valueless.

Labelling and Care of Collections

Labels

Labels are of two distinct types, one giving the name of the specimen and the other, known as the data label, giving the other available information, such as the name of the locality where it was taken, the date of capture and the name or initials of the collector.

It is a matter for your own choice how you arrange your collection and what labels you apply. As your collection grows it will need constant rearrangement, which forms interesting work for the winter months. You may suddenly find a liking for one particular group, or even breed a very long and varied series of a single species which requires more room. Do not lay out a box or cabinets too fully with a lot of labels and hope to catch the specimens later. It is better at the beginning to expand and rearrange as you go along, and you can then see where subsequent events and interests lead you.

You will soon learn to group specimens into families, and once you have definitely identified a specimen, you can give it its family or generic name, which is in Latin and which always begins with a capital letter; this is followed by its species or specific name, which always begins with a small letter. For a number of groups you can place English names underneath as well, but the more uncommon groups of insects have not been given them.

It is better not to paste labels in your boxes for you will want to move them about from time to time as the collection expands. It is usual to pin them in with small pins or headless stainless-steel points. The more important label is that giving the data, for without these details a collection is quite valueless to anyone else and has no scientific value.

I have of course met collectors who refused to place any labels on their specimens, on the grounds that they made the collection purely for their own enjoyment and knew when and where they caught everything. This is rather a selfish attitude, for the specimens would be of no real use to anyone else.

A proper data label should give on the top line the country of origin; the name of the county appears below, and beneath this the place of capture. The fourth and last line contains the collector's name and initials.

A second label should give the date of capture or remarks such as 'bred'. Where mountains are involved and the height is of importance, this is often given by a mere figure such as 2,000 ft (600 m). Where applicable 'light', 'light trap' or even just 'M.V.' is added.

Collectors who confine their collections to specimens caught in the British Isles use many short cuts. Many give county, place and date only. Some omit the county and add their name. In England it has long been the custom to place an asterisk on a label – this signifies 'bred' and is in general use.

Whatever you decide upon NEVER number specimens and keep the information in a book. The number of collections I have seen where this has been done is enormous, and in nearly all cases the owner has died and no one can find the key which unlocks the vast store of knowledge he has filed away. It is more understandable in collections of minerals where the specimen is rough or powdery and cannot be labelled unless in a small box of its own; but for an insect on a pin to have no label at all is a serious omission on the part of the collector.

Storage boxes

I have seen beginners start their collection of butterflies or other insects with nothing more than a good-quality chocolate box with a well-fitting lid and a few wine corks cut into slices and glued in the bottom of the box in rows. This, though not making a good display, is perfectly good storage, especially if you glue one or two naphthalene balls in the corners to keep out any mites.

Under certain conditions insects will keep indefinitely and specimens over a hundred years old are quite common. The two essential requirements are dryness and either very air-tight boxes or a suitable preservative, regularly renewed, to keep away mites, etc.

On your setting boards insects may be exposed, since at this stage they are drying out. Bodies of moths, especially large ones, will smell at this stage, though this is not perhaps detectable by the

LABELLING AND CARE OF COLLECTIONS

collector. This means they will be attractive to clothes moths, museum beetles or mites. You can help to ward off trouble by keeping them in a drying house or cardboard box with some insect deterrent, but there is one precaution you should always take. Never transfer straight from your setting boards to a permanent storage box or cabinet or you may introduce an infected specimen and the trouble may spread. You should always have a half-way house which is used for temporary storage and for sorting insects before fixing their final data labels.

The early storage boxes used by pioneers do not differ greatly from those in use today. They were often, however, disguised as books by having a rounded back or spine covered in leather or cloth and often lettered with some learned-sounding title. As mentioned earlier, collecting was considered a little mad at first – hence the disguise. This disguise was later fostered by many of the clerical profession, who – being educated men, often with an interest in natural sciences, and with time off in the day for following up this interest in a practical way – made some of the finest early collections.

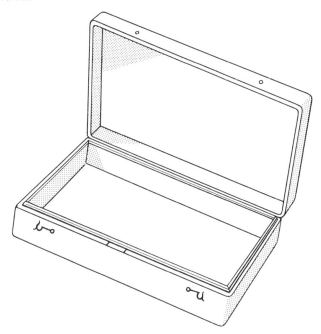

Fig. 39 Insect storebox

STUDYING INSECTS

This book arrangement and the sizes of library shelves seem to have controlled the sizes of storeboxes. In my earliest catalogue – one by William Watkins dated 1894 – the sizes are given as 10 × 8, 14 × 10, 16 × 11 and 17½ × 12 in. He also offered the same in 'book pattern', though in this case the second size was given as 14 × 10¼. The price of the largest box (ordinary style) was then 6s! The sizes, with the exception of 16 × 11 in., are those made today, but now the price of the largest box is about £3.00.

An insect storage box is fairly simple to make now that composition cork is available. Formerly virgin cork was used in storeboxes and cabinets; it was cut to size and then jigsawed in, sanded down and papered.

Later, virgin cork became scarce and cork linoleum was substituted. Second-hand boxes lined with this can be detected by their extra weight. They work well, but the pins come out with a slight jerk, which often causes the bodies of insects to come off.

The advantages of storeboxes are that they are cheaper than cabinets and can be easily rearranged on a shelf to allow for gradual expansion of the collection. The chief disadvantages are that they can be dropped or jarred more easily, and when they are opened their close fitting causes a slight inward rush of air which can loosen the wings of insects. This last disadvantage, however, will also occur with certain cabinets. All storeboxes should have a flange running round inside (Fig. 39) and a camphor cell.

Cabinets

New cabinets are very expensive, but fortunately those coming on the market second-hand seem to keep pace with the demand; there are generally enough about, although you might have to wait a little longer for certain patterns or sizes. The two cheapest styles have drawers with plain glass lids which either drop in or slide in a groove. These are perfectly good if proper care is taken with insect deterrents (see page 107). The better types of cabinet have the glass fitted into a lifting-off frame lid and built-in camphor cells.

There are generally two types of drawer suspension, one having wooden rails on which the drawers run and a joining rail across the front under each drawer. The second is the hidden bearer method, where the rail is still on the side of the cabinet but runs in a groove in the side of the drawer. This means that the front joining rail under each drawer is not required, and in consequence the cabinets will not be so high.

LABELLING AND CARE OF COLLECTIONS

The great point to watch for when choosing a cabinet is to make sure that the drawers will all interchange easily. This is a help when adding to your collection since they can then be rearranged.

A system adopted by the British Museum (Natural History) is to have the floors of the drawers made from thin sheet metal. Long slats of thin wood, covered with sheet cork and papered, run from front to back of the drawers. They can vary in width according to the group of insect housed. This arrangement enables one slat to be used for each species, which makes rearrangement and expansion of a collection very easy.

Another method which is gaining ground in America is to have the sheet-metal base as before but to fill the drawers with small, varied, rectangular white cardboard boxes, each lined with sheet cork on the bottom and papered over. This also allows rearrangement, and the species under examination can be removed completely and the whole series examined under a microscope. Another point in its favour is that if a body or part of an insect becomes accidentally detached it will be found in the card box with the specimen and not loose in a drawer with possibly a second body, making it difficult or impossible to decide which belongs to which specimen. This method is of course for small insects and not butterflies or very large insects.

On the Continent, where long thin pins are used, boxes and sometimes cabinets are lined with thin blocks of peat into which the pins will enter without bending. These boxes are finished by papering the sides first and then allowing about $\frac{1}{2}$ in. (12 mm) of paper to turn on the bottom and lie on the peat all round the box. Since you cannot get the paper covering the bottom to stick to peat, this paper is dampened first and then pasted round the edges only on to the $\frac{1}{2}$-in. (12-mm) border; when dry it stretches tightly across the peat.

The drawback to these boxes is noticed only by those who have to work on small insects with a microscope. A pin will leave a small hole. When you remove a specimen, the paper will grip the pin slightly and be drawn away from the peat before coming free and dropping back. This makes a perfect powder bellows and fine dust from the peat is puffed out through old pinholes. It may only be microscopic, but work with a microscope and you will see what I mean!

New linings of plastic foam material have recently been tried, but they are not yet reliable. The holes made by pins do not close

STUDYING INSECTS

up when the pin is drawn out. The plastic contracts slightly and unevenly with age and it also becomes harder.

Balsa wood will probably take the place of peat for those who must use long thin pins, but these pins are a hangover from the past. Many continental museums now stage small insects on polyporus pith, but old systems die hard.

Some time ago a new system of insect cabinets was introduced. This was the unit system and consists of a base, a middle section of ten drawers and a movable top. The idea is to add to your collection by inserting a new section, and it is feasible to go as high as thirty drawers before you expand sideways. This system is quite good for smaller museums and even for the larger private collections, but there are one or two drawbacks which those who started on the system years ago have now discovered. Though secondhand cabinets come on the market from time to time, the new ones are at the moment made by one firm only, and labour costs are so high that new units are very expensive. This forces up the price of second-hand ones to nearly the same figure, so those collectors who have saddled themselves with this system have either to pay the price or give it up. Other cabinets are available second-hand at half the price.

Fig. 40 Insect cabinet

LABELLING AND CARE OF COLLECTIONS

Another minor disadvantage is that in the days of cheaper housing collectors could often have their own 'den' when a museum appearance was an asset. Today, however, cabinets are often an integral part of the furnishing of a room, and there are many beautiful old cabinets in a great variety of styles which will fit into most rooms without strong objections from the distaff side of the household. In my opinion nothing looks so attractive as a well-matured and polished cabinet of about twenty drawers or less (Fig. 40).

Converting or reconditioning cabinets or boxes

Many collectors either make their own cabinets or more frequently convert a cabinet made for another purpose for their own entomological use. If you are converting a drawer which has no glass, it is not generally possible to fit lifting-off frames to hold the glass. This would add to the height of the drawer, which of course would prevent you from putting it back in place unless you could rehang the whole set of drawers by moving the position of the runners; but you might then be left with a drawer out to allow for the extra lid space required and almost certainly with an odd space left over at the top or bottom of the drawers. In addition frame-lid making is rather advanced carpentry, like picture-frame making, and unless you are confident of a good result, it is better to leave it well alone.

This leaves you with two alternatives, a sliding-out or a drop-in glass lid. You cannot groove the sides of a drawer once it is made up, and in any case you would have to lower the back to allow the glass to slide out, so this system is not really practicable. The best idea – which incidentally provides better protection against insects – is to fix drop-in glasses. You can fix in beading about $\frac{1}{4}$ in. (6 mm) below the top of the drawer on all sides and cut your glass to a good fit. You will either have to cut a small slot at the back of the drawer or fix a short tape to allow you to raise the glass to open the drawer for use.

This idea works well, but the beading on which the glass rests is not easy to cover with paper and looks clumsy. It is far better to insert a wooden fillet right down to the base of the drawer and this is easily papered. Another advantage is that you can leave out a section of this fillet, and when papering the side go right across the gap. This will then leave you with a built-in camphor cell, and you need only prick a few holes in the paper to allow the fumes of your naphthalene to enter the drawer (Fig. 41).

STUDYING INSECTS

Sheet composition cork is available and a stock size is 3 × 2 ft (91 × 60 cm); it is often cheaper to buy one of these cut to a convenient size than have sheets cut to measure. You will be charged for wastage anyway and you can always use your own off-cuts for something else.

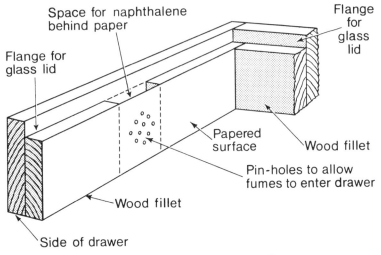

Fig. 41 Converting an ordinary drawer for use as an insect cabinet

You should not cork tight to the edges of the drawers but leave about $\frac{1}{16}$ in. (2 mm) clear all round. This helps slightly when papering and also removes any risk of the cork sheet humping up when you are gluing it in. You need not have your cork sheet all in one piece. Jigsaw odd pieces in if you have to, but before papering use glass paper on a flat block of wood and smooth down any discrepancies in the level of the joins. Cork sheet is generally sold already sanded on one side, and it is done with a precision machine; this saves a great deal of work, so always specify sanded on one side when ordering your supply.

Papering and repapering

Many collectors boggle at papering, which is really a simple task if you know what to do. The majority either make a bad job of it or take an easy way out which I do not recommend, namely whitewashing the insides of the drawers on top of old, dirty paper.

LABELLING AND CARE OF COLLECTIONS

There was a period during and just after the last war when good paper was not available; paper might look white but would turn yellowish rather quickly, and possibly brown. In this case it might have been as well to whitewash, but today good-quality paper is available – by which I mean white art paper from a good supplier and maker, not cheap drawer-lining paper for household use.

The whitewash used was generally a mixture of zinc oxide and water, and there are some old formulas for this in books. Some advise the adding of a little glue and 'bluebag'. Zinc oxide used to be very cheap, and the better alternative, titanium dioxide, was expensive. During the wartime hunt for metals to stand the great heat developed in rockets, vast deposits of titanium were discovered, and today titanium dioxide is cheaper than zinc oxide, which has risen in price. The titanium preparation also has a property of great use in cosmetics: its covering power is extremely great and since it is a pure white a very thin layer indeed will cover perfectly. These chemicals, of course, stay white since they are already oxides, whereas paper on exposure to air will gradually turn yellowish or brown.

A box or drawer looks well if done carefully without ridges or brush marks, but you can never be sure the whitewash won't flake off, and in any case it comes off on your hand if you rest it on the floor of the drawer to steady it when pinning in a specimen. Water added to a drawer covered with one of these oxides simply goes into a number of beads and owing to capillary action rolls about, picking up a little powder but not soaking the paper until much later. You can immediately stop this with a few grains of any of the modern washing detergents. Just sprinkle them in the drawer and the beads of water collapse and unite.

It is easiest to soak off the base of old papers first. Plenty of water may be added, but this has to soak right through the paper – there may be more than one layer – and soften the paste underneath. Leave it nearly an hour before you lift out the old paper. If you don't, you will scrape and scrabble for hours and end by gouging out holes in the cork.

Some cabinets may have the paper fixed in by thin glue or size. Before lifting out the soaked paper, drain off any water and add a little scalding hot water straight from a kettle. The paper will then lift off at once. You will have to wipe out the drawers afterwards with hot water and a sponge to remove any traces of glue, and then sponge dry.

STUDYING INSECTS

Now turn the drawers on edge and soak the sides. These will not soak easily when the drawers are flat and if you turn them on edge and deal with one side at a time, you will keep the water from creeping under the cork and softening the glue. This takes longer, but you can do all the drawers at once.

You must allow the drawers to dry out completely. This may seem silly if you are to add a wet paste, but you must avoid any risk of the cork or glue in the joints getting wet for too long and you must have a dry surface for the next stage, a light rub-over with glass paper on a wooden block before new paper is added. You must then, of course, dust the drawers out, a job which is better performed out of doors.

When papering the drawer you first cut out the sheet for the bottom, allowing about $\frac{1}{4}$ in. (6 mm) extra all the way round. Carefully noting the position from which it was cut, wet it all over to see on which side it will expand. Having noted this, cut your side pieces, which are for the longer sides of the drawer; they should be the exact depth and about $\frac{1}{2}$ in. (12 mm) longer. For these you can use paper which expands lengthwise when wet. Then cut the pieces for the shorter sides of the drawer, using paper which will not expand lengthwise since the pieces will have to be an exact fit. Cut them the exact depth of the drawer, minus a very small fraction to allow for sideways stretch, and the exact length.

The bottom sheet is pasted in first, and turned up all round the edges; the two longer sides next, each corner turning slightly. Finally the two shorter ends are placed in, which exactly fit. You will then have no joins showing in your paper at all. When cutting, use a razor blade and a long ruler and do a number of sheets in one operation.

For paste use a dry paperhanger's powder which is mixed with cold water. It takes a minute or two to take up the water and expand to the right degree; add water as you mix and then leave it to stand and add more water if required. With practice you can avoid lumps!

Prepared paste or thin glue is not advisable. The glue hardens the top of the cork and like the prepared paste is inclined to be hygroscopic and will absorb damp. This means your pins may well corrode at paper level and break off, leaving points in the cork. It may take years to happen, but be warned in advance.

Having first covered your table with layers of newspaper, wet the paper on the wrong side – there always is one though it is not

LABELLING AND CARE OF COLLECTIONS

readily visible. Use plenty of water and a clean brush. Allow at least five minutes for the water to soak in and stretch the paper. Then brush off any surplus water and evenly paste it all over. When placing the paper in, you should dab it all over at first rather than wipe a cloth across or along its edges. If you do wipe it in this way you will drag it slightly at the edges and when it is dry you will have a lot of small ridges along the sides of your drawer. This is a fault all amateurs make and is not too easily avoided.

When you attempt to wet the narrow strips for the sides you may find these curl up. To avoid this, wet your sheet of newspaper all over, then place the strips on and wet them, when they will all stay flat.

After papering you should allow a day or two in a warm room for complete drying out before shutting your box or closing up the cabinet lids.

Grease and degreasing

Some insects have a tendency to become greasy after a little time in storage. This means that the fat content in the body starts to spread and grease appears on the body and later spreads to the wings, giving these an oily and sometimes almost transparent appearance. This does not always happen since insects which have flown for some distance have used up this fat, and migrants from the Continent are almost free from a fat content.

Some species are more prone to this disfigurement than others. The Red Admiral butterfly is one and the Eyed Hawk and Puss moth are the two moths most likely to turn greasy. Some collectors say that moths caught by sugaring are more likely to turn greasy, especially if they have had a good feed on the sugar patch.

An early symptom of grease is sometimes a tuft of a green hair-like substance which appears round the pin where it enters the body of the insect, either on top or underneath. This is verdigris and is a compound formed by the grease and the brass content of the pin. It is the reason for using plated or enamelled pins, though the grease will sometimes eat through this protection. If you spot this in the early stages you can repin the specimen with a stainless-steel pin, but if you leave it too long the green substance will form crystals inside the thorax of the specimen and ultimately split it wide open.

When repinning, first remove the data labels. Grip the point of

STUDYING INSECTS

the old pin in such a manner that the underside of the insect's body is between the tips of your finger and thumb. Then grip the head of the pin in your forceps. If the pin is corroded too badly you may break the pin at once, but try to rotate the pin head, which should free the pin inside the insect's body.

You can now start to withdraw the pin by pulling it out with the forceps and holding the thorax of the insect down with a pair of straight-ended fine forceps resting lightly on either side of the pin. Never try to extract a pin without first turning it round to free it, or you may break open the thorax and the moth will disintegrate.

There are several ways in which to degrease a specimen. One is to rest it on a small bed of fuller's earth and sprinkle a little more on the top and over the wings. Leave it for about two weeks and on removing it gently blow away any remaining dust. This takes time but has one great advantage over other methods in that the fringes on the wings are not matted.

The other methods are similar to one another and only the various chemicals used are different. The method is to soak the specimen in a small jar of degreasing agent or solvent. The best is toluene, but you can also use carbon tetrachloride, ethyl acetate or benzene.

It is a good plan to have three baths of fluid ready, A, B and C, and leave the specimen for about two days in each. If you have a lot of specimens you can throw away bath A since this will have removed the most grease; you then add a clean one at D. If you cannot find a good jar and have a large insect such as a Hawk moth, you can use an old tongue jar. Grind the top flat as described on page 80 for flower-pots, and cover with a piece of glass.

When lifting out the specimen after degreasing, you should first examine the surface of the fluid. Small beads of brownish oily substance may be floating there, and this will be the fat extracted from the insect. Skim this aside with a piece of blotting-paper and lift out the specimen from a clear patch.

On immersion all colour disappears and the insect becomes almost transparent. When the specimen is taken out of the fluid, the colour returns as it evaporates. The evaporation takes place very rapidly and you should have a small blow-pipe ready. With this blow gently on the fringes of the wings and around any fluffy parts of the thorax. This will make the insect dry even more quickly and leave it with an unmatted appearance.

If you have a rare specimen it is a good plan to snip off the ab-

LABELLING AND CARE OF COLLECTIONS

domen with fine-pointed scissors while the insect is still on the setting board and then soak the abdomen as described. Just before you remove the insect from the setting board, glue the body back in place, and the board will help to hold it steady during this operation.

Some years before the last war M. Mactaggart bred a very remarkable series of Pine Hawks. These distinguished themselves and their fortunate owner by emerging black, white and creamy. My father at once advised degreasing the bodies, which in this species are resinous owing to the nature of the food plant, and this was carried out.

During the war, when the attention of their owner was elsewhere, the cabinet of specimens was badly attacked by museum beetle and only pins, dust and labels remained – except in the Pine Hawk drawer where the specimens were all perfect. Having no grease content they were unattractive to the pests and were left untouched, and this fine series is now in the Cockayne-Kettlewell Collection in the British Museum (Natural History), London.

Repairing damaged specimens

There is one group of insects I dislike handling very much once they are set and dried and in cabinets and boxes. This is the order covering grasshoppers, locusts, mantids and stick insects. They all have rather large and cumbersome legs and even when alive, as you may have experienced, grasshoppers shed their legs with very little provocation. They are even worse when dead. If the legs are glued on again they still seem to come off almost as easily, possibly owing to their size and position which make them liable to catch in anything close by. The answer is to use a rubber solution or a similar preparation. Place some of it on each surface and allow it to dry for about ten minutes; if you then bring the two surfaces into contact you get an immediate bond. The substance, however, always retains some of its elastic properties, so that when a leg is next caught it will give way a little as if actuated by a muscle, and will not just drop off.

The abdomens of most Lepidoptera are also likely to come off from time to time when you are rearranging your collection; even when alive they are held by a mere thread. You can glue these back again with several types of gum, but make a support from a narrow strip of thin paper in the shape of a V with two side arms resting lightly on the insect's wings. This will support the body in the correct position while drying (Fig. 42).

If you are unfortunate enough to dislodge a wing, you must turn the specimen upside down on a setting board and get the wings, including the loose one, firmly secured with setting tapes. You can then add a little glue just where the wing joins the thorax.

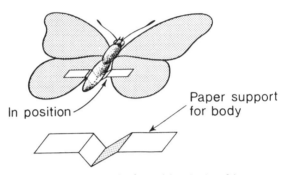

Fig. 42 Method of repairing body of insect

When making a scientific study the condition of specimens may not always matter. Perfect ones are desirable but a damaged one is better than none, for it will still have the structural features of interest to the taxonomist. For a collector not so scientifically minded, whose collection is a thing of beauty and has a sentimental value, a butterfly with a piece out of one wing, but otherwise intact, must be restored to a perfect appearance. This can be done by inserting a similar piece, slightly larger, from the corresponding wing of another insect, using it as a patch. The type of fixative used must be studied since all except one, as far as I know, shrink slightly on drying; on the amount used and the position the wing is in, depends the amount the wing will curl up or wrinkle as the gum or fixative dries. Watkins & Doncaster market a wing-repairing fixative which is absolutely non-shrinking when dry. It is best to use a minute quantity of this on a pin and touch it round the edge of the hole to be repaired, on the underside of the wing, then bring the new patch up to it from underneath, making sure to get the alignment of veins and pattern correct before you finally press it home. This method will patch a wing so perfectly that the patch is often invisible to the naked eye.

Another type of repair which I dislike having to make is that of the long bodies of dragonflies. If the specimen has been kept in the dark and starved for about a day before killing, as mentioned earlier, the body will be a better colour. It will also not have decayed internally and these specimens seem to be stronger.

Others, however, will break very easily, leaving you with a hollow tube, the walls of which are so thin that there is nothing to put gum on, and when you do reattach the fallen section it breaks in a fresh place. I have seen specimens mended by collectors who have inserted a long thin pin or a piece of wire inside the whole length of the abdomen. I use a thin piece of polyporus pith; this can be rounded by pressing it with the fingers, especially if it is a soft piece. It can also be compressed to the correct diameter, but I have to colour it before use. This material is extremely light in weight and also flexible, but there may be a better method which I have yet to be shown.

Insect deterrents

The expression 'camphor cell' is the one in common use to denote a cell or compartment designed to hold some sort of insect deterrent. Though camphor has been used in the past it has a strong tendency to make those insects that are inclined to turn greasy become so more quickly. Confusion is also caused by shops calling naphthalene balls 'camphor balls'. The two substances are quite distinct.

Naphthalene balls can be used in a box, but rather than just glue one in, it is safer to wrap it in fine muslin and then pin it. An alternative method is to heat a stout pin in a flame and when it is practically red-hot, plunge the head into a naphthalene ball. It will melt its way in rapidly and the melted portion will solidify within a few seconds and seal it in. The ball can then be pinned in. There is, however, nothing more distressing than seeing a loose ball make a track through a box of insects as you tip the box up. It is better to use flaked naphthalene. This is safer and also, having a much greater surface area, gives off stronger fumes. Naphthalene will keep insects away and also lasts a long time. If you have attacks by museum beetles, mites, etc., or suspect them, use crystals of paradichlorbenzene as this will actually kill them, but remember that it evaporates quickly and don't go abroad and leave a collection with only this in it. Naphthalene is much safer for a long-term policy.

If you overdo the quantity of naphthalene in a cell and your room suffers a sudden drop in temperature after being warm, small crystals of naphthalene looking like hoar-frost may form on the wings and bodies of your specimens. Don't try to remove this. Expose the specimens to the air and it will soon evaporate, and then you can reduce the quantity in your cells.

Mould

If specimens are put in store before they are dry, or your boxes are kept in a damp room, mould may form on the bodies. It is always a good plan to add specimens to your cabinet on a warm day or in a warm dry room. Mould forms on the bodies first but if left alone will spread to the wings.

Fig. 43 Glass cell for anti-mould fluid

Mould can often be removed from the wings of butterflies with a camel's-hair brush. If a dry brush won't work, try one dipped in carbolic acid (phenol). When lifting mould from insects, don't forget the scales overlap on the wings and bodies like tiles on a roof, so work along in the direction in which the scales lie so that you do not dislodge them and so damage the appearance of the specimen.

You cannot use a chemical fluid for removing mould on a butterfly which is an iridescent blue, such as a male Adonis Blue. It will discolour the wings permanently.

Mould can be prevented considerably by the use of beechwood creosote, a clear oily fluid which smells like ordinary creosote and can be purchased from almost any pharmacist. Only a very few drops need be used, and don't forget it is oily and may stain the floor of your box or cabinet. You may be able to tuck it away out of sight on a little cotton wool in your camphor cell, but an alternative is to obtain some of those compressed cotton-wool balls which are thrown about at carnivals and dances. These can be mounted on a long pin and pinned into one corner of your drawer. A more costly alternative is a glass cell (Fig. 43).

If your cabinet drawers do not run smoothly, you can use one of the modern silicone wax polishes on the sides. This is much more efficient and cleaner than using graphite which has been the custom in the past.

Ants

MAKING A FORMICARIUM

Ants, of the order Hymenoptera, are to be found almost everywhere and can be the subject of very interesting study.

There is no need to say much about catching ants except for the special method required later, but keeping them in captivity is well worth your attention. A home-made ants' nest or formicarium is quite an easy item to construct if you carry out the following instructions carefully.

You require a cardboard-box lid about the size of a shoe-box. Next cut a sheet of glass 1 in. (25 mm) narrower than the lid and $\frac{1}{2}$ in. (12 mm) shorter. Place your lid flat on a table with the edges uppermost and insert the glass sheet. This should touch one end and when placed correctly will have about $\frac{1}{2}$ in. (12 mm) of space round the remaining end and two sides.

Next make a number of plasticine 'worms' not quite so thick as a pencil. Arrange these worms on the glass in any kind of pattern. Don't get them too close to one another and don't let them cross. If one meets another, cut the end and join it on to the side of the other worm. At the end where the glass does not touch the lid place on the glass a small block of wood about 1 in. (2 cm) square and 3 in. (8 cm) long. Your chain of worms must link up with this at the two ends (Fig. 44), and you can also make a few shallow blobs of material here and there.

Mix a large bowl of plaster of Paris, enough to fill your box lid completely, making sure to add the plaster to water and not vice versa; pour this over and smooth it off level with the edges of the box lid. When your plaster has hardened, peel away the box lid, gently prise up the sheet of glass and remove the plasticine worms and wood. This must be done carefully so that you will not break away pieces of plaster.

If you then replace the sheet of glass you will see that you have a box or block of plaster with a large chamber at one end, a number of passages, and a few smaller chambers here and there. You should now check to see that the sheet of glass is clean and will slide away at one end. This is the end that touched the end of your box lid and the object is to allow you to slide the glass to give access to the large chamber at the opposite end.

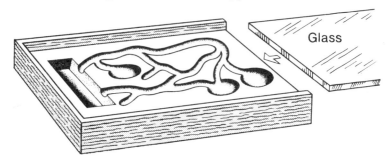

Fig. 44 Formicarium

Collecting stocks

Your formicarium is now ready for stocking with ants; there are many species you can keep in this way, but I am chiefly concerned with something practical for the beginner.

Look for a nest of the Red Ant (*Myrmica laevinodis*); these are usually found in meadows and waste grassland, nearly always under flat stones, pieces of old iron or other objects which are not too thick. A heavy, thick object will not allow the sun to warm the nest, which is essential if the ants are to thrive. If you locate one of these nests, remove the stone or other covering and replace this with a large sheet of smooth slate. It may take a few days for the ants to settle down under this new roof, and you must hope no one else interferes with it in the meantime.

You now need a fairly deep rectangular tin with a clean smooth inside. This is for collecting your stock of ants, and as you require a number for a healthy stock, and picking them up one by one is too slow, the reason for the sheet of slate will now be obvious. Wait for a warm day when your ants' nest will be active and the ants not all underground. When the sun is warm it is safe to assume that a great many ants will be on the underside of the slate, so have your tin ready and quickly raise up the slate. You can then make several quick scrapes and the ants will fall in your tin. You will only have time to do about three scrapes before they start climbing out, so give your tin a final shake to make all the ants fall to the bottom and then replace the lid.

It is important for the health of your colony to include a queen, and that is the reason for starting with this species of ant. There are always several queens to a nest, and one will almost certainly be included on the slate. If you miss it you can look for one later. It will be very much larger than the workers and quite easy to discover.

You have now to introduce your colony into the formicarium and you start by sliding back the glass so that the large chamber at the end is uncovered. If the tin is jarred firmly the ants will lose their grip and fall to the bottom. They will then grasp anything and in fact will form a loose ball. With a final quick tap after you have removed the tin lid, shoot them all into the formicarium and slide back the glass sheet before they can run about and escape.

Try to exclude all earth when collecting ants since if any is introduced in the formicarium they will use it to line the passages, and particularly to cover the tops of the tunnels so that you cannot see what is going on. You must now remember the golden rule, NEVER raise the sheet of glass. If you do, the ants will be all over the top of the plaster of Paris in a flash and you will never manage to lower the glass back into position without crushing many of them, and even then it won't sit flat. Always slide the glass so that all passages remain sealed at the top.

From time to time you might have to clean out the largest chamber, which will no doubt be used by the ants as a rubbish tip and even as a cemetery. To do this without losing ants, wait until the chamber is unoccupied and then slide back the glass and insert two plugs of cotton wool in the two tunnels leading off the chamber. You can then do what is required.

Having installed your nest, cover all the glass with a thick sheet of cardboard to keep it dark, but leave the large end-chamber exposed. An elastic band will hold this card in place, and it is removed only for observation. Water should be placed in the chamber, and sugar water is the best; this can be placed in the upturned cap of a toothpaste tube. You will also have to maintain humidity in the nest and this is done simply by adding a teaspoon of water in the large chamber and, if you think it is required, more on the plaster at the sides. The plaster soon absorbs the moisture and distributes it evenly. If your nest is too dry, the ants will rush to the damp spot and start sucking the moisture up.

STUDYING INSECTS
Feeding

While sugar and water will keep ants alive, as in the case of most other insects in captivity you will also have to supply more food, especially if you have grubs and want to rear the brood through all its stages, which is necessary if your colony is to survive and flourish. The best food for ants is meat in the form of small caterpillars and even other insects. You can place these in the chamber, and by trial and error learn what is acceptable to them. Choice food, such as a small caterpillar, will soon be dragged well into the nest and later a small piece of dried skin and the head will be carried out and heaved over among the rubbish. Chopped-up worm will also serve as meat, but only a very small amount is required at a time. Moth pupae are also accepted, but you have to open them slightly before placing them in the formicarium. The smaller chambers are necessary and you will find that one of these will be occupied by the queen, another by her brood and another by ants' 'eggs', which are of course the pupae.

Ants can be hibernated in one of these formicaria by allowing the food supply to fall lower and letting the nest get cooler. They can be stored in a cold cellar, but you will have to watch the moisture content. They must not be allowed to dry out. All being well, they will congregate in a huddle for warmth in one chamber and remain inactive for the winter months. If, however, you are confident you can keep the food supply going, you can keep your nest active. There will be some remarks later (page 128) on breeding stocks of insects in captivity for food supplies, research, etc.

Don't be alarmed if in the first few days after you have stocked your formicarium the death-rate appears high. Several ants will get damaged during the collecting, and these will die or be killed off by other workers and be discarded from the nest. Keep your food supply as regular as possible. If you allow this to get too low, the ants will start to eat their brood and undo weeks of work.

Besides the method of collecting a nest just described, you can also dig one out and collect grubs and a stock of workers, but you must always make sure of a queen. If schools require something rather more ambitious, you can make an open nest of wood ants surrounded by a wide trough of water on all sides. Several pounds of the woody nest material are collected at the same time, and in this case you will not be able to see the workings of the nest since it

ANTS

will be covered over as in the wild state. The same hints about food apply on a larger scale, and these ants will also accept ripe fruit from time to time.

There is a new substance on the market called Fluoron which is the result of recent research by I.C.I. If you can obtain some, you can use it to confine ants.

Take a large open container with steep sides and, near the top, smear an uninterrupted band of Fluoron about $\frac{5}{8}$ in. (15 mm) wide. Ants will go up to this band, but will not cross over it, so are nicely confined. This band will last quite a time but personally I am a little afraid of using it for a long period. It is possible that dust may adhere to it, or a fragment of something may blow on to it, and thus make a bridge which the busy ants will not take long to find. It is, however, ideal for an exhibition of short duration, or for demonstrations in a classroom. Its one great advantage is that it is portable; it is not easy to carry about a tray of ants surrounded by a moat full of water.

Wasps in Captivity

Wasps, another group of the order Hymenoptera, are only too easy to collect, but they also form an interesting group for study and it is a fairly simple matter to keep a captive nest in the house. The life cycle is well known. In the autumn the nest produces a large number of male and queen wasps which leave the nest on a nuptial flight. The fertilized queens then disperse and hibernate, while the remainder of the nest dies when the cold weather commences.

The hibernated queens each start their own nest in the spring and you must look for one of these, which will be quite small. The first or nucleus nest is about the size of a golf ball and is made entirely by the queen. Inside will be a small piece of comb with perhaps nearly twelve cells. The queen lays an egg in each and will forage for food to feed the grubs, often getting killed in the process, for you often find these small nests without an owner.

When the grubs have matured and hatched, the queen will have about a dozen workers and will now no longer leave the nest but will leave the task of foraging for food and nest-building material to the workers. She will remain behind, but will help in enlarging the nest and finally become nothing more than an egg-producing machine.

If you find a small nest you can catch the queen and workers, if any, and keep them in a box while you transfer the nest to an observation box. I find a wooden tube about 1 ft (30 cm) square and 18 in. (45 cm) long is ideal. This has open ends and you suspend the little stalk at the top of the nucleus nest from the roof of the wooden tube with a drawing-pin. It should be placed more or less in the centre. The wooden tube should now be placed on a shelf in front of a small ventilator window and the window opened. Place a sheet of glass across the end of the tube nearer the window. This is only temporary, but should be tight enough to keep wasps in. Release the wasps into the other end of the tube, when they, or the queen as the case may be, will fly to the light and be stopped by the glass. They may find the nest at once, or you may even have to give the queen a prod in the right direction. Once they find the nest they will enter and see if everything is all right. When this happens you can remove your pane of glass and hope for the best. It is unlikely that the queen or any workers will fly out of the end of the wooden tube which is towards you, for they will go towards the light.

If all goes well the queen will leave, make a recognition flight outside the house so that she can find her way back, and then return with nest material or food for her small brood. You can then observe the comings and goings for the rest of the season. This activity will not fill your kitchen with wasps since the workers will fly straight out of the nest for some distance before hunting for food and it is most unlikely that any will trouble you. You will be able to stand quietly immediately behind the nest and watch its construction.

The two most common species of wasp make different nests, that of *Vespula germanica* being grey and fairly strong and that of *Vespula vulgaris* being brown and rather crumbly. Either may be kept in captivity as described. You may even substitute a queen of one species for a queen of another, first cutting off her wings. This will not hurt it and is exactly what happens to queen ants when they commence a new nest. When the workers of the new queen mature, they will naturally try to make their own colour nest and at first you will have streaks of different nest. As the older workers die out the nest will become all one colour but different from the original.

A great advantage in keeping animals of this kind is that they feed themselves. Don't shut your window or they will die rapidly from lack of moisture. I once trapped many thousands of worker wasps to obtain the poison from the sacs behind the stings. This was required for research into the drugs contained in the poison. I used a copper gauze tube with a funnel turned in at one end and a lid on the other. This was placed over the exit hole of a nest at night. Next day the tube would be full but had to be removed before midday or the wasps would all be dead from lack of moisture.

It was interesting to note other specimens which entered the trap from the nest. I frequently found spiders, quite untouched by wasps, and late in the season a rare beetle and species of Diptera

STUDYING INSECTS

parasitic on or scavenging in the nest. The wasps in the trap do not seem to interfere with other occupants.

On the bottom of the wooden tube containing your captive nest you will find a gradually increasing heap of rubbish formed of waste-food particles, cast larval skins, etc. In this you will find larvae of various Diptera which can be bred out. At the end of the season the nest will gradually empty itself. As the number of workers diminishes, the remaining wasps cannot cope with the larvae, and they carry these from the nest and drop them outside, so that you can ultimately dry the nest and keep it to show others. The heap of waste matter with its larvae can be transferred to a flower-pot half filled with sand and a sheet of glass placed on top as described earlier. You will need to damp this at about the end of May, when some interesting flies will emerge.

Finally a hint on tracking wasps back to their nest, either queens in the spring or workers later on. If you dice up some cooked white fish into cubes about $\frac{1}{8}$ in. (3·1 mm) in size, the wasps will remove this. The idea is to give it a load it can just carry, so adjust the size of the cubes accordingly. When the wasp picks one up in its mandibles it will return to the nest but will only be able to fly very slowly, and the white dot going through the air can be followed by the eye. If it goes a long way, mark its flight and then stand some distance along the line of flight and watch for another to come along. This is then tracked a stage further and may lead you to the nest.

Humble-bees

You cannot, unfortunately, go out and collect a wild nest of one of the humble-bees. It is so difficult to achieve this that I don't advise anyone to attempt it. In addition, you may destroy several possible nests, and this little group of insects are extremely useful to have about, if only because they work such long hours. A raspberry crop is almost impossible without the help given by humble-bees in fertilization.

If you can locate a wild nest in your garden or on ground where no one else will interfere with it, you can do a great deal to assist the queen with her nest and at the same time turn it into an observation nest. Several of the Bombus family, which have the very large furry queens so conspicuous in the spring, will make their nests in holes in the ground, and others will use an old bird's nest or a site in thick gorse to which they will add moss to make a firm nest. This latter kind of nest can be transferred to a nesting-box rather like that used by tits, but the ground-nesting species are more satisfactory for observation.

The queen hibernates during the winter months, and on waking searches for a suitable nesting site. These are almost invariably the old holes used by longtailed field mice or field voles; in fact, the nest of a field mouse with its fine shreds of grass lining a small cavity is a ready-made nest for a humble-bee. If you can locate one of these nests you should wait until the queen goes out foraging before you meddle with it. Try to find how far it goes into the ground, and in what direction, by inserting a thin bendy twig. Having decided this, carefully dig away the top soil until you uncover the cavity. After making sure it is a proper nest and not just a hole that the queen was exploring, cover the top of the cavity with a fairly large and solid piece of tile or similar material. It is essential that this should keep out the light and also any surface water which might flood the nest.

STUDYING INSECTS

Since the hole was probably that of a mouse in the first instance, this will mean that a mouse can get right down it. There is nothing so attractive to a longtailed field mouse as a pot of honey with a few grubs to go with it. There are two ways of keeping them out. You can wait until the queen is inside and then cover the outside with about 1 sq. ft (0·09 sq. metres) of the finest-gauge wire-netting, pegging it well down and covering all of it, except that actually across the mouth of the hole, with the surrounding natural material. The queen will come out and possibly make a recognition flight round the entrance, and all being well she will return.

The second method is less disturbing to the queen. A small piece of wood through which you have made a queen-size hole is inserted across the nest tunnel about 4–5 in. (10–12 cm) inside; it should be done when the queen is out foraging, and you should disturb the natural entrance to the tunnel as little as possible. This should act as a mouse excluder.

In the early stages of nesting the queen humble-bees have to contend with the weather. There will be very wet days or even long cold spells which will confine the queen to the nest. The nest at this stage will be little more than one or two cells, perhaps one full of pollen, another containing some honey, and possibly one or more with an egg or young grub.

Even later on the nest continues in much the same manner, but a group of cells have grubs and some are capped with domes under which are pupae waiting to emerge as adult insects. Old cells are brought into use as spare honey pots. In the bad spells of weather the queen will be forced to eat into her small store, which was really gathered for her expected brood. You can greatly help her, if not save her life, by lifting your nest cover and dropping a teaspoonful of honey into a cell.

Besides the humble-bee family there are others which you can entice into the garden by providing suitable nesting sites. You can provide a ventilating brick which has holes about the size of a pencil. These bricks can be stood on edge so that the holes are horizontal, and covered with a slightly overhanging roof of two pieces of plank to provide shelter. The bricks should be in the sun and, with luck, mason and plasterer bees will occupy the holes.

A Sub-terrarium

The title of this device is almost self-explanatory, and it was first devised by the late Hugh Main. The sub-terrarium (Fig. 45) consists of a wooden frame of a base and two sides only usually about 9 in. (23 cm) long and 6 in. (15 cm) high. The frame holds two sheets of glass and the distance apart can be adjusted. The sheets of glass are covered on the outside by sheets of black paper to exclude any light; the paper is supported by cardboard to prevent crinkling, and an elastic band is placed round the whole so that the glass can be easily removed when you wish to examine the frame.

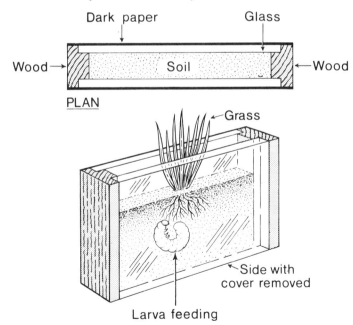

Fig. 45 Sub-terrarium

STUDYING INSECTS

Between the glass you place earth, peat or ground-up rotten wood as the occupant of the apparatus may require. The secret of operating one of these successfully is to adjust the two panes of glass so that they are far enough apart to allow your specimen to move between the glass freely, but not so far as to allow it to conceal itself in the earth or other material.

This type of cage works very well for stag-beetle larvae, which otherwise frequently die on exposure and are very hard to rear. Use powdered rotten wood in this case, and keep it fairly damp. The pupation and emergence of these huge beetles is seldom witnessed unless you have a device of this sort. I have also used it for fully developed larvae of one of the largest burying beetles, and for larvae of the cockchafer or may bug, but with the latter you must have grass or other roots growing in the top. Keep your frame out of the sun, which would cause undue condensation on the glass; the hints given on page 75 on mould can be followed here if necessary. This apparatus is very simple to make and is of great use in schools and to those who wish to watch insect development in all its stages and to photograph it at the same time.

Illustrating Insects

You may need to illustrate an insect or part of an insect. The whole insect when photographed may make a good picture, but it also may not be suitable if you require to reproduce the whole of it exactly, since the thorax is not in the same plane as the wings which makes it difficult to get both these parts in a proper focus. If you wish to photograph living insects which are flying about or sitting on flowers, this can be made easier if you get some stiff wire – about 3 ft (91 cm) is ideal – and fix a length under your camera. At the distant end you bend it about 3 in. (7 cm) upwards. You then focus your camera on the tip of your wire rod. When in use you only have to keep the wire tip under the flower head or under the insect, if it is flying about. There is no need to look into the camera. Every time the insect is over the tip it will be in focus, so just watch it carefully and press the button (Fig. 46).

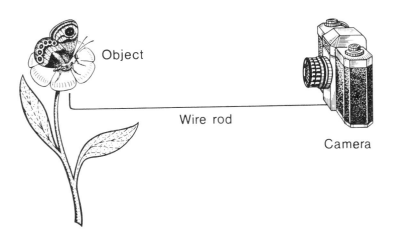

Fig. 46 Photographing living insects

STUDYING INSECTS

It is more likely you will need to draw or illustrate in some way only a particular part of an insect and there are several ways this can be done.

You can insert into a microscope a graticule, which is a very thin slide divided into very small squares. By using a drawing paper with printed squares you can draw your insect part, using the squares as a guide. By using larger squares on your paper you can get a larger picture if required.

You can also use a camera lucida which is a simple piece of apparatus which you clamp on the top tube of your microscope. One part consists of a hinged mirror which can be adjusted at various angles and this, if you are right handed, should extend to the right of your instrument. Under the mirror you place your drawing paper. When you place the tip of your pencil on the paper you should be able to see it when you look through the microscope, and then all you have to do is to draw round your magnified object (Fig. 47).

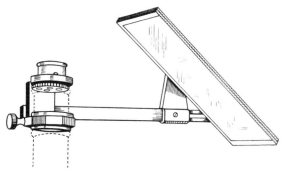

Fig. 47 A camera lucida attachment

The disadvantage of this system is that it requires a little practice to get it correctly in focus and, secondly, that unless you have everything nicely arranged you get a distorted picture, and one part will be longer than another.

This camera lucida has been in use for a very great many years with little attempt at improvement. Today we have a modern microscope with a built-in camera lucida which is simple to use and extremely accurate, and can be used with a choice of four magnifications. The disadvantage is the price which is beyond the purse of most people but perhaps you will be able to borrow one from some institution or persuade a society to which you belong to

ILLUSTRATING INSECTS

buy one for members' use. It is mentioned here so that you may know that this microscope is available to the serious student (Plate 14, below).

Messrs Flatters & Garnet used to make a good projecting apparatus which was later improved and altered considerably, but this too became very costly. One of the early types is shown here (Plate 15, above) and if you cannot obtain one second-hand, it is not beyond the skills of a handyman to reproduce, but by using a wooden bar instead of metal. The apparatus is a microscope with a mirror on the end where your eye would normally be. Next comes a holder for your slide or object, then a lens. In the photograph is a glass container filled with water to absorb the heat from the lamp. This can now be replaced by buying a heat-absorption lens which is available. Lastly there is the light source. In the photograph this is concealed, but it is merely a car head-lamp bulb. This apparatus will reflect downwards on to your paper so that you can draw round the picture quite easily.

Finally, you can photograph your insect or insect part, and this is made simple today by a fairly inexpensive attachment that you place on the top of your microscope (Plate 15, below). There is a screw to hold it on and at the top there is an adjustable ring to fit various cameras. An elastic strap holds it secure. At the side there is a single eyepiece which enables you to watch the focus while operating the camera and no light can get in by way of this eyepiece. You need a good light on your object, and you can produce this by using an ordinary bull's-eye condenser. Black and white photography is quite cheap so you can do a trial run with different lighting and examine your negatives before you have them printed.

Attracting Butterflies and Moths to your Garden

The varieties of butterfly and moth to be found in your garden depend a great deal on the type of soil, and consequently the type of food plant, to be found in your district. The list of moths you obtain may be very much larger than you would have suspected, since the first lesson learnt from the use of mercury vapour moth-traps was that moths normally travel far greater distances during the course of their natural comings and goings than was at first thought. We already knew that moths migrate and that species fly to England from Africa or even further, but local breeding species were at first thought to keep very much to their birth-places and the food plants in that area.

The moths found on pine trees provide a striking example of mobility, for although the nearest area where pines grow may be some two or three miles away from your house, species feeding on pines will be found in a mercury vapour trap in your garden. When I first installed one of these traps in the Zoological Gardens at Regent's Park, it was placed on the corner on top of the reptile house. Although it was already mid-July seventy-four different species of larger moth were recorded before the end of the season.

Except for the migrating species, butterflies are very much more restricted, by natural habit, to one quite small area. This means that the number of kinds visiting your garden may be small, but also that species liberated there will stay with you if there are attractive plants and shrubs on which they can feed and somewhere for them to roost. A good forester will clear ivy from trees and most gardeners do this, but if you leave one tree covered in ivy or one fairly high clump of ivy you will not only provide the perfect roosting place for both butterflies and moths but also, when it is large enough to flower and produce berries, a breeding place for the pretty Holly Blue butterfly. Butterflies will roost in thick ivy and if confined by long spells of wet weather will crawl to the edge of the underside of a leaf and extend their tongues for a drink. This kind of ivy will also attract the large pale-yellow Swallow-tail moth and its larvae, which you can beat. They are fine examples of 'stick caterpillars'.

Large clumps of ivy also act as suitable places for butterflies to hibernate. I have a tree which is used for this purpose, and in the autumn I remove what spiders I can from the ivy by attracting them from their hiding-places with a tuning-fork. The fork is struck and then just touched to a leaf. The noise is exactly like a fly in a web and the spider dashes out. In mild winters spiders are on the move for longer periods and this must play its part in reducing the numbers of hibernating insects which are then an easy prey.

The first bush attractive to insects in the spring is the sallow – the male tree with the fine big fluffy yellow catkins, not the female with the smaller green ones. This tree is easily grown from a cutting; if you take one, select a tree at catkin time, choosing a good stem with buds as small as possible and not a piece in flower. There is just time for this to take root, but keep it well watered, especially if you get dry weather later on. The sallow catkins will attract moths at night and hibernating butterflies such as Peacocks, Red Admirals, Small Tortoiseshells and the Commas – not forgetting, in some districts, the Large Tortoiseshell. (The Red Admiral is also a migrant.) A spring-flowering rockery with colourful plants may attract and provide food for butterflies.

The next shrub which is attractive is the orange buddleia, *Buddleia globosa,* with the sweet-smelling orange balls. This is very easily taken from a cutting, but, unlike the other species of buddleia, does not like being pruned.

Buddleia alternifolia is a very attractive shrub for butterflies and most ornamental in the garden. It will flower quite early and is best grown as a standard. When you prune, leave the long hanging growth of new wood and trim away all the minor growth and old wood. Later you can follow with other buddleias – the common blue and mauve forms, the powerfully coloured royal red, and, if you are able to find one, the pure-white variety.

Buddleias will produce several feet of new shoots each year and will stand any amount of pruning. They also take easily from cuttings and you can use quite large long shoots for this, both in spring and in autumn. If you prune too early in the spring, the new growth is likely to get damaged by frost, but it is always worth pruning one bush in the autumn and trusting to luck. This will flower earlier in the year and by pruning others at intervals you get a succession. You can also grow one as a pot plant and use it for butterflies in laying tubs, since cut buddleia does not last in water.

By keeping the pollen from the spring-flowering orange buddleia and storing it in a refrigerator, nurserymen have crossed this with the later-flowering purple kinds. Few nurseries list the hybrid, but it is of great value to the entomologist. The flower is a compromise, being a long spike but made up of balls. The flowering time is late September or October, according to your pruning, and it is valuable as a final feed for butterflies which have to build up before hibernating for the winter.

The only disadvantage of this interesting hybrid is the colour, which, although bluish when in bud, is tea colour when open, so that the shrub looks rather withered. Because of this, butterflies do not readily find it, but it is most attractive to queen humble-bees and to moths at night, when of course colour is of no consequence.

During August there is *Senecio clivorum,* a cultivated variety of ragwort with large leaves and a fine flower spike with large orange flower heads arranged one above the other so that it lasts a long time. I have seen this plant in the water gardens at Sandringham during August so smothered in Red Admirals that there was hardly room for one more. There are other varieties of this plant, such as *Senecio clivorum desdemona,* with a redder flower, which I have not yet tried.

Fennel, *Foeniculum vulgare,* is worth growing to attract insects. It is the food of the Swallow-tail butterfly when in captivity but the females will not lay on it. On new soil it may grow too tall in the first year but after that it will become smaller and of a convenient height for observing insects.

Finally, in the autumn, don't forget the Michaelmas daisies. All varieties are attractive to butterflies, but I find they prefer the very short varieties of 9–10 in. (23–25 cm) now available. These do not wave about in the wind and disturb them; they can shelter from the wind on a lower plant and feed in comfort.

You can now breed butterflies and liberate them in your garden, where they will stay until it is too cold and they are forced to hibernate. The top half of my tool-shed is left open at one end and I always have a few butterflies hibernating there each winter, generally among old wooden seed or other boxes stored among the rafters.

If your garden is large enough or you have a farm or estate, you

ATTRACTING BUTTERFLIES AND MOTHS

will even find clumps of stinging-nettle a source of attraction. Unfortunately a weed-control spray is now available which actually mentions on the tin and in advertisements that it will kill nettles: the perennial variety, generally found on waste ground not suitable for cultivation – often piles of old bricks in farmyards, heaps of stones, or where there were formerly buildings. If you see nettles sprayed anywhere you should make it your duty to point out to the offender that five of our most beautiful butterflies will feed on this plant and that today they are not so abundant as formerly.

There are a few more plants which will attract moths and other insects at night. The tobacco plant, now available in many colours, has a powerful perfume at night which attracts the Convolvulus Hawk moths; these hover over the flowers and extend their very long probosces into the flowers. Honeysuckle can also be obtained from nurseries in cultivated varieties and can be grown over arches or up poles. There are other plants, but the rule is to have them very sweet-smelling.

Insect Cultures

I am frequently being asked which insects, if any, are suitable for breeding in large numbers all the year round. These are required for use in laboratories for testing insecticides or other research work, or possibly merely for use as food for a pet chameleon or lizard.

The choice of insects is not very large, but I strongly advise those who require insects for feeding purposes to have at least three varieties breeding at the same time. This will give a change of diet. Small amphibia are soon bored by receiving the same food day after day, and with some species inanition can set in with fatal results. When the moth trap mentioned on page 124 was started at the London Zoo, the reaction of certain animals to a sudden and varied change of diet was very noticeable. Not only did they seem to wake up but they also ate more, being tempted by a wider variety of food and by more active food. An insect on the move is much more attractive to an animal, which will not only notice it but will possibly make an automatic grab for it before it gets out of reach. Insects bred in cultures are often extremely torpid on emergence and simply sit about.

The chief rule for cultures is to remember to start clean ones at frequent intervals. Take a clean cage and a fresh stock of food from a different source and introduce adult insects only, with no odd food particles from your old stocks. If you don't do this you may lose your stocks from some disease or overdose, or acarine mites which are practically invisible.

The following specimens are useful for breeding continuously. They are given in order of size of the adult, smallest first.

Fruit-fly (*Drosophila*)   Diptera
House-fly (*Musca domestica*)   Diptera
Blow-fly (*Calliphora*)   Diptera

INSECT CULTURES

Meal moth (*Ephestia kuehniella,* also known as *E. sericarium,* the Mediterranean Meal Knot-horn)   Lepidoptera
Honeycomb moth (*Galleria mellonella*)   Lepidoptera
Mealworm (*Tenebrio molitor*)   Coleoptera
Garden Tiger (*Arctia caia*)   Lepidoptera
Common cockroach (*Blatta germanica*)   Orthoptera
African locust (*Schistocerca gregaria*)   Orthoptera
Migratory locust (*Locusta migratoria*)   Orthoptera

The Fruit-fly is extremely common in warmer weather when, of course, cultures must be started. Merely leave some over-ripe bananas or pieces of melon about and you will soon attract it. (Bananas are available all the year round, but you should keep your fly stocks warm while breeding.) Heat and light (which is radiant warmth) may be provided by an electric light bulb suspended in a fairly large cage. In all cases mentioned here the bulb should not be too close to your breeding stocks. This species is used extensively in laboratories and may be used to demonstrate genetics.

The House-fly is much more difficult to obtain since in some districts it is becoming rare owing to the use of D.D.T. and other chemicals. It will feed on many substances, but most people feed it on moistened bread. A little experimentation is needed by the beginner before he learns by trial and error the food that is just right. The bread must not become too wet or too fermented.

The blow-fly is one of the easiest species to breed, but often rather smelly. You only have to expose meat in warm weather and you will get all the eggs you need at once. There is one tip you can adopt which makes the task cleaner and more pleasant. You require a wooden tray with a perforated zinc mesh on the base – not the standard mesh but one with large holes. This should be stood flat on a sheet of cardboard and the food placed in the tray. The cardboard is to prevent the maggots from falling through when very small. When they are fully developed, raise the tray about an inch over a second tray containing some clean sawdust, and remove the cardboard. The top tray can be removed and you will have a stock of pupae in reasonably clean conditions.

Heat and light are required to keep stocks going all the year round. If, however, you merely require some adult flies for a short time, almost any fishing-tackle shop will supply you with a few pence worth of gentles, as these are called, and you can hatch them out. They will require a little moisture and warmth to pupate properly and you will find some may not be fully grown when purchased.

The Meal moth is common in nearly every corn store. Most proprietors will deny that they have any insects in their stores and you will have to make a tactful approach. If there is an outside store with grain and various types of meal spilt on the floor, so much the better. The amateur will not know the moth he is looking for, but if you rake among the loose meal you will find long tubes of fine web with particles of meal adhering to the sides. These tubes will contain the larvae or pupae you want and can be collected and transferred to a cylinder type cage with a stock of fresh food. Warmth will be required all the year round but light is not necessary. The greyish moth expands to about 1 in. (25 mm). In some flour mills the webs have been known to choke the machinery.

The Mealworm is found under similar conditions and the larvae look like those of the wire-worm, being brown and stick-like. The rearing conditions are the same as for the Meal moth, but although the Meal moth will do well on porridge oats, the Mealworm will thrive better on something with a little meat content, such as crumbs of dog biscuits, mixed in with meal.

The Honeycomb moth is a little larger than the Meal moth; it also has a larger body and consequently a fatter larva. It feeds on old honeycomb, brood cells and waste matter cleaned from hives. It will get into hives and was once a menace when the old type of woven hives were in use many years ago. You may have difficulty in obtaining stocks unless you can get in touch with someone who is keeping a culture of this moth. It will breed all the year round if kept warm and it too does not require any light.

A little experience with cultures will show that it is always possible to have several going with development in each at a different stage so that you have a constant supply of adults or larvae as required. You can expedite this at the beginning by halving your stock and keeping one half warmer than the other to hasten it on, while cold will retard the other half.

The Garden Tiger, which has the 'woolly bear' caterpillars, can be caught as an adult or collected as an almost half-grown larva on dead nettle and other low-growing plants in the spring. In captivity it will become continuous brooded if kept in the dark in a warm place and fed on cabbage. Cardboard shoe-boxes are very suitable since they will avoid condensation when kept warm, and the cabbage leaves keep fresh enough if cut off and added daily. Care will be required with larvae of this sort to avoid disease. You must discard any sickly looking larvae, or any which fall behind the others in development. A number will not respond to your efforts to break their diapause and will try to hibernate; I usually discard these too for safety. Use clean boxes frequently and burn old boxes, especially those in which adult moths have emerged. When emerging, these moths carry a large amount of meconium, the fluid excreted by the moth (or butterfly) to aid its emergence from the chrysalis. Any surplus fluid, which is generally pink in colour, is shed, and it can carry disease to your next brood.

Cockroaches are found where heat and food are available, in such places as large hotel kitchens and ships' holds. This is no reflection on hotels; the insects are in many London buildings and extremely hard to get rid of completely, for the young nymphs can get right into crevices and along pipes into cavity brickwork.

They are a useful species for work in schools as they are large enough to handle and dissect. They can be bred in captivity if kept constantly warm, but lights are not required. These insects have long legs and longer antennae so they require a lot of space, which may be obtained by using a cylinder type cage and putting in a number of thin shelves; these may be glued together by connecting pieces of wood to form a single unit. The shelves may be made of thin plywood cut in circles or hexagons and spaced about $\frac{1}{4}-\frac{1}{2}$ in. (6–12 mm) apart. Enough space should be left round the sides of the cylinder for the cockroaches to move about freely. This arrangement gives a very large surface area, for they will use both sides of the discs. On the top you can place shallow saucers of food – oatmeal, cake crumbs, sugar and cereals. Cockroaches also require water. Elaborate heating arrangements can be avoided if you are able to place them close to a hot tank in a cupboard or in a boiler room. The larger species, *B. orientalis,* may be kept in the same manner, but they are not quite so easy to manage and your initial stocks will be much harder to obtain.

Locusts are easy to breed but require much more heat, and light is also required, so that light bulbs may be used to provide both. They can be reared in a cylinder type cage with clean sand in the bottom. Fresh grass, if possible with roots attached but shaken free from soil, is added daily. They will lay their long egg purses in the sand, but you must at once separate eggs from adults and keep all your nymphs of one size together, for larger ones will eat smaller ones. The adults will require twigs to climb about and sit on, and these should be placed at a low angle against the cylinder side to allow the adults to hang down for wing development.

Thanks to modern insecticides the Bed Bug (*Cimex lectularius*) has been almost wiped out in this country but is rampant in places overseas. From time to time many of these bugs are wanted for research on pesticides and it is worth mentioning here that they can now be very easily reared by keeping them in a shallow container over which is stretched a very thin rubber membrane. Blood given by donors and stored in hospitals is only kept for a period and then becomes 'out of date'. This blood is normally discarded but it is ideal for rearing *Cimex*. You will need to invert a bottle of blood against the rubber membrane and raise the temperature of the blood to that of the human body or very slightly higher. You can do this either by winding a rubber tube round your container and letting warm water from a tap run through it or by using a small aquarium immersion heater. The bugs will pierce the membrane with their stylets in order to feed.

Identification of Insects

Collecting anything is not much fun if you cannot put a name to what you find and do not know therefore if it is considered rare or not; and there is no doubt that the ease with which you can name something has a very great influence on what is collected. A number of collectors may later become serious students or scientists and may discover fresh fields where names are not so vital, for they will find new species and give them their own names.

For many years insect collectors were largely concerned with butterflies and a few of the moths, chiefly because the only books available were about this group. Even today the highest proportion of collectors and serious students is concerned with moths, butterflies coming second. Beetles come next but now, since the publication of *Flies of the British Isles,* by Colyer and Hammond, the Diptera or two-winged flies are receiving much more attention. A very small proportion of entomologists concern themselves with dragonflies, bees and wasps, grasshoppers, caddis-flies and lacewings, and even fewer with parasitic Hymenoptera or the ichneumon flies and their smaller associates.

Identification for the beginner often means getting a book with coloured plates and matching up the specimen. He will be at a loss, of course, when he catches a rare migrant, a foreign introduction or a melanic (black) variety. Then the more serious student who studies the wing venation and structure of the specimens will have the advantage.

The following orders are now, for the British Isles, covered by popular works giving coloured plates of most, if not all, of the species: Lepidoptera, Coleoptera, Hemiptera-Heteroptera, Diptera and Odonata. Of the Hymenoptera, bees and wasps have also been well illustrated. Less attention, however, has been given to the parasitic Hymenoptera, which may well prove to be the largest and most important group in the British Isles, although it may be many years before it is sorted out and named.

STUDYING INSECTS

The chief reason for the comparative neglect of the parasitic Hymenoptera has been the very small size of the greater proportion of its species, and this order will serve to illustrate the method used in identification. The beginner will sort his specimens by an almost casual glance, and if he is concerned with butterflies or dragonflies, for example, he will not go far wrong. The more serious student or advanced collector will realize that orders have been created because groups of insects all have the same major characteristics, particularly in the formation and structure of their wings.

Very small Hymenoptera cannot be identified by pictures for several reasons apart from the labour and vast expense. Many are extremely alike and the microscopical differences would not be apparent in an illustration of the complete insect. These small differences are often allied to bigger differences in the internal structure. Linnaeus, the first to attempt classification of natural life and the inventor of our present system, recognized a small black parasitic fly and having given its approximate size described it in one Latin word *Niger*. We know now that there are some two hundred species under the same genus and they are nearly all quite black. Small insects such as this are classified in the first instance by their wing structures and there are publications which show these very clearly.

Orders are, in some cases, divided into sub-orders, and then into super-families and families. The families are divided into genera and each genus into species. The wings serve to distinguish the genus in most cases.

Identification keys consist of series of couplets differentiating between features which will separate groups from each other, for example, between genera and then the species in each genus. Let us assume that you have already used a key to put a specimen in the correct genus.

The couplets in a series are numbered consecutively from 1 onwards, and there is another number alongside the second line of each couplet. If the first line of the couplet agrees with the specimen you are examining, you proceed to the next couplet. Let us suppose that the key for the species begins by saying 'colour entirely black', and on the next line 'colour not entirely black'. You then examine your specimen and see, perhaps, that half of the abdomen is banded with an orange-red colour, so you refer to the number alongside the second line of the key. Supposing this to be 20, you

IDENTIFICATION OF INSECTS

pass on to couplet 20. This might say 'basal half of the abdomen coloured red, remainder black', and you will realize you are on the right track. The following couplet (21) might refer to measurements of parts of the insect, such as 'second joint of the antennae longer than the first' and 'not so describable'. You then re-examine your specimen and decide that this time the first line agrees with what you are examining, so you proceed to the next couplet. Finally, when there are no more differences separating specimens, you will reach a point where you can go no further. If your specimen agrees with everything up to this point, the name will be found alongside the last couplet. You may, however, find further small differences so you will be looking at a new species.

The Royal Entomological Society has published a series of handbooks each of which deals with a separate group of insects. These works all use keys but are also illustrated, and the illustrations help to explain the terminology.

One of the objects of this book is to encourage the amateur and help him to bridge the gulf which separates him from the scientist. The inability to name specimens and the slightly awesome appearance of technical publications often make the less expert collector avoid the more difficult groups, although it is in these fields that the most interesting new discoveries lie and that more workers are required. There is no need to be intimidated by a key; you will have to learn the names of insect parts used in the key, and the rest is a matter of trial and error.

APPENDIX I

A Code for Insect Collecting

JOINT COMMITTEE FOR THE CONSERVATION OF BRITISH INSECTS

This Committee believes that with the ever-increasing loss of habitats resulting from forestry, agriculture, and industrial, urban and recreational development the point has been reached where a code for collecting should be considered in the interests of conservation of the

STUDYING INSECTS

British insect fauna, particularly macrolepidoptera. The Committee considers that in many areas this loss has gone so far that collecting, which at one time would have had a trivial effect, could now affect the survival in them of one or more species if continued without restraint.

The Committee also believes that by subscribing to a code of collecting, entomologists will show themselves to be a concerned and responsible body of naturalists who have a positive contribution to make to the cause of conservation. It asks all entomologists to accept the following Code in principle and to try to observe it in practice.

1. *Collecting – general*
1.1 No more specimens than are strictly required for any purpose should be killed.
1.2 Readily identified insects should not be killed if the object is to 'look them over' for aberrations or other purposes: insects should be examined while alive and then released where they were captured.
1.3 The same species should not be taken in numbers year after year from the same locality.
1.4 Supposed or actual predators and parasites of insects should not be destroyed.
1.5 When collecting leaf-mines, galls and seed heads, never collect all that can be found; leave as many as possible to allow the population to recover.
1.6 Consideration should be given to photography as an alternative to collecting, particularly in the case of butterflies.
1.7 Specimens for exchange, or disposal to other collectors, should be taken sparingly or not at all.
1.8 For commercial purposes insects should be either bred or obtained from old collections. Insect specimens should not be used for the manufacture of 'jewellery'.

2. *Collecting – rare and endangered species*
2.1 Specimens of macrolepidoptera listed by this Committee (and published in the entomological journals) should be collected with the greatest restraint. As a guide, the Committee suggests that a pair of specimens is sufficient, but that those species in the greatest danger should not be collected at all. The list may be amended from time to time if this proves to be necessary.
2.2 Specimens of distinct local forms of macrolepidoptera, particularly butterflies, should likewise be collected with restraint.
2.3 Collectors should attempt to break new ground rather than collect a local or rare species from a well-known and perhaps over-worked locality.

CODE FOR INSECT COLLECTING

2.4 Previously unknown localities for rare species should be brought to the attention of this Committee, which undertakes to inform other organizations as appropriate and only in the interests of conservation.

3. *Collecting – lights and light-traps*
3.1 The 'catch' at light, particularly in a trap, should not be killed casually for subsequent examination.
3.2 Live trapping, for instance in traps filled with egg-tray material, is the preferred method of collecting. Anaesthetics are harmful and should not be used.
3.3 After examination of the catch the insects should be kept in cool, shady conditions and released away from the trap site at dusk. If this is not possible the insects should be released in long grass or other cover and not on lawns or bare surfaces.
3.4 Unwanted insects should not be fed to fish or insectivorous birds and mammals.
3.5 If a trap used for scientific purposes is found to be catching rare or local species unnecessarily, it should be re-sited.
3.6 Traps and lights should be sited with care so as not to annoy neighbours or cause confusion.

4. *Collecting – permission and conditions*
4.1 Always seek permission from landowner or occupier when collecting on private land.
4.2 Always comply with any conditions laid down by the granting of permission to collect.
4.3 When collecting on nature reserves, or sites of known interest to conservationists, supply a list of species collected to the appropriate authority.
4.4 When collecting on nature reserves it is particularly important to observe the code suggested in section 5.

5. *Collecting – damage to the environment*
5.1 Do as little damage to the environment as possible. Remember the interests of other naturalists; be careful of nesting birds and vegetation, particularly rare plants.
5.2 When 'beating' for lepidopterous larvae or other insects never thrash trees and bushes so that foliage and twigs are removed. A sharp jarring of branches is both less damaging and more effective.
5.3 Coleopterists and others working dead timber should replace removed bark and worked material to the best of their ability. Not all the dead wood in a locality should be worked.
5.4 Overturned stones and logs should be replaced in their original positions.

STUDYING INSECTS

5.5 Water-weed and moss which has been worked for insects should be replaced in its appropriate habitat. Plant material in litter heaps should be replaced and not scattered about.

5.6 Twigs, small branches and foliage required as food plants or because they are galled, e.g. by clearwings, should be removed neatly with secateurs or scissors and not broken off.

5.7 'Sugar' should not be applied so that it renders tree-trunks and other vegetation unnecessarily unsightly.

5.8 Exercise particular care when working for rare species, e.g. by searching for larvae rather than beating for them.

5.9 Remember the Country Code!

6. *Breeding*

6.1 Breeding from a fertilized female or pairing in captivity is preferable to taking a series of specimens in the field.

6.2 Never collect more larvae or other livestock than can be supported by the available supply of food plant.

6.3 Unwanted insects that have been reared should be released in the original locality, not just anywhere.

6.4 Before attempting to establish new populations or 'reinforce' existing ones please consult this Committee.

The Joint Committee for the Conservation of British Insects was set up in 1968 through the good offices of the Royal Entomological Society to absorb and fulfil the functions of the Society's own Conservation (Insect Protection) Committee. The representative basis of the Committee was broadened to include all the national entomological societies, and the Committee itself invited individual entomologists to represent the interests of particular regions of the country. The Committee is now independent of the Royal Entomological Society as far as its freedom of action is concerned, but is supported administratively by the Society.

The Committee's activities have included the publication of an account of the value of dead and dying wood in the conservation of insects, the consideration of species of Lepidoptera for introduction or reintroduction, the evaluation of the entomological importance of threatened sites, the examination of the status of species thought to be endangered and the preparation of lists of species at risk. It hopes to include all aspects of insect conservation in Britain in its future work. The Secretary is Dr M. G. Morris, c/o Royal Entomological Society of London, 41 Queen's Gate, London, S.W.7.

Reprinted by kind permission of the Royal Entomological Society of London and *The Entomologist*.

APPENDIX II

Times of Appearance of British Butterflies

The times of appearance of butterflies in their various stages are given in the following table. Unfortunately there will be variations in this table according to the weather for the year. A long fine spell in the spring will advance the table by as much as two weeks. Continued fine weather will cause caterpillars to feed up faster, and in exceptional years some species which are usually regarded as single-brooded will consequently have an extra brood while others will run to three broods. A fine autumn often extends some species to three broods. One year I took a White Admiral in September which had only just emerged some days after I had seen a third brood of the Wood White. This extra brood is partial and represents only a small percentage of the brood, the remainder of which emerge at their normal time. It is unlikely that confirmed single-brooded species, such as the Brimstone, Hairstreaks, Camberwell Beauty, Large Blue, Large Tortoiseshell, Marbled White, Orange Tip, Peacock, Purple Emperor and one or two of the Skippers, could produce second broods, even with artificial aids; consequently their times of appearance are more constant.

If this appendix is used in conjunction with Appendix III, you can search for eggs or larvae according to the season.

TIMES OF APPEARANCE OF BRITISH BUTTERFLIES

o = *ova*   l = *larva*   p = *pupa*   i = *imago*

	J	F	M	A	M	J	J	A	S	O	N	D
Adonis Blue	l	l	l	l	pi	li	p	pi	li	l	l	l
Bath White	p	p	p	p	li	l	p	pi	lp	p	p	p
Black Hairstreak	o	o	o	o	l	lpi	i	o	o	o	o	o
Black-veined White	l	l	l	l	lp	pi	li	l	l	l	l	l
Brimstone	i	i	i	i	li	li	pi	pi	i	i	i	i
Brown Argus	l	l	l	l	l	p	pi	i	l	l	l	l
Brown Hairstreak	o	o	o	o	l	lp	pi	i	i	o	o	o
Camberwell Beauty	i	i	i	i	i	l	lp	i	i	i	i	i
Chalk Hill Blue	l	l	l	l	lpi	lp	pi	i	l	l	l	l
Chequered Skipper	l	l	l	l	p	i	o	l	l	l	l	l
Clouded Yellow	—	—	—	—	i	li	lp	i	li	lpi	i	—
Comma	i	i	i	i	li	lp	pi	li	pi	i	i	i
Common Blue	l	l	l	lp	i	il	li	i	i	l	l	l
Dark Green Fritillary	l	l	l	l	l	lp	pi	li	l	l	l	l
Dingy Skipper	l	l	l	lp	i	li	lp	i	l	l	l	l
Duke of Burgundy Fritillary	p	p	p	p	pi	iol	l	l	lp	p	p	p
Essex Skipper	o	o	o	ol	l	p	i	i	o	o	o	o
Gatekeeper	l	l	l	l	l	lp	i	i	l	l	l	l
Glanville Fritillary	l	l	l	lp	lpi	lpi	l	l	l	l	l	l
Grayling	l	l	l	l	l	lpi	pi	li	li	l	l	l
Green Hairstreak	p	p	p	p	pi	li	lp	p	p	p	p	p
Green-veined White	p	p	p	pi	li	lpi	lpi	lpi	lp	p	p	p

STUDYING INSECTS
TIMES OF APPEARANCE OF BRITISH BUTTERFLIES – (Contd)

o = *ova* l = *larva* p = *pupa* i = *imago*

	J	F	M	A	M	J	J	A	S	O	N	D
Grizzled Skipper	l	l	l	lp	i	li	lp	i	l	l	l	l
Heath Fritillary	l	l	l	l	l	lpi	li	l	l	l	l	l
High Brown Fritillary	l	l	l	l	l	lp	pi	li	l	l	l	l
Holly Blue	p	p	p	pi	i	lp	pi	li	lpi	lp	p	p
Large Blue	l	l	l	l	l	li	i	l	l	l	l	l
Large Copper	l	l	l	l	l	pi	i	il	l	l	l	l
Large Heath	l	l	l	l	l	pi	i	l	l	l	l	l
Large Skipper	l	l	l	l	lp	i	i	iol	l	l	l	l
Large Tortoiseshell	i	i	i	i	io	l	lpi	pi	i	i	i	i
Large White	p	p	p	pi	li	lpi	lpi	li	lp	lp	p	p
Long-tailed Blue	—	—	—	—	—	—	—	i	i	—	—	—
Lulworth Skipper	o	o	o	o	l	lp	pi	i	o	o	o	o
Marbled White	l	l	l	l	l	lp	pi	io	l	l	l	l
Marsh Fritillary	l	l	l	l	lpi	lpi	l	l	l	l	l	l
Mazarine Blue	—	—	—	—	—	i	i	—	—	—	—	—
Meadow Brown	l	l	l	l	lp	pi	i	li	l	l	l	l
Milkweed	—	—	—	—	—	i	i	i	i	—	—	—
New Clouded Yellow	—	—	—	i	i	li	lp	i	li	lpi	i	—
Orange Tip	p	p	p	pi	li	li	lp	p	p	p	p	p
Painted Lady	i	i	i	i	i	li	lp	lpi	li	i	i	i
Pale Clouded Yellow	—	—	—	i	i	li	lp	i	li	lpi	i	—
Peacock	i	i	i	i	io	iol	lp	pi	i	i	i	i
Pearl-bordered Fritillary	l	l	l	l	i	lpi	lpi	l	l	l	l	l
Purple Emperor	l	l	l	l	l	lp	pi	l	l	l	l	l
Purple Hairstreak	o	o	o	o	l	lp	pi	o	o	o	o	o
Queen of Spain Fritillary	—	—	—	—	—	i	i	i	—	—	—	—
Red Admiral	i	i	i	i	i	li	lp	lpi	i	i	i	i
Ringlet	l	l	l	lp	lp	lp	lpi	l	l	l	l	l
Scotch Argus	l	l	l	l	l	p	pi	i	l	l	l	l
Short-tailed Blue	—	—	—	—	i	lp	i	i	—	—	—	—
Silver-spotted Skipper	o	o	o	o	l	lp	pi	i	o	o	o	o
Silver-studded Blue	o	o	o	o	l	lp	pi	i	o	o	o	o
Silver-washed Fritillary	l	l	l	l	l	lpi	i	oli	l	l	l	l
Small Blue	l	l	l	l	pi	il	lp	il	il	l	l	l
Small Copper	l	l	lp	l	l	pi	i	li	lpi	l	l	l
Small Heath	l	l	l	l	lpi	lpi	lpi	lpi	l	l	l	l
Small Mountain Ringlet	l	l	l	l	lp	pi	i	o	l	l	l	l
Small Pearl-bordered Fritillary	l	l	l	l	i	lpi	lpi	l	l	l	l	l
Small Skipper	l	l	l	l	l	lp	pi	l	l	l	l	l
Small Tortoiseshell	i	i	i	i	li	lpi	pi	li	pi	i	i	i
Small White	p	p	p	pi	i	li	pi	i	lp	lp	p	p
Speckled Wood	l	l	lp	pi	i	l	lpi	i	l	l	l	l
Swallow-tail	p	p	p	p	pi	li	lpi	lpi	p	p	p	p
Wall	l	l	l	lp	pi	l	lp	i	l	l	l	l
White Admiral	l	l	l	l	lp	pi	il	l	l	l	l	l
White Letter Hairstreak	o	o	o	o	l	lpi	pi	i	o	o	o	o
Wood White	p	p	p	pi	pi	l	p	li	lp	lp	p	p

APPENDIX III

Food Plants of British Butterflies

WITH NOTES ON THE EGG LAYING OF CERTAIN SPECIES

Adonis Blue	Horse-shoe vetch
Bath White	Mignonette, horse-radish
Black Hairstreak	Blackthorn (sloe)
Black-veined White	Apple, blackthorn, hawthorn, plum
Brimstone	Buckthorn (all species)
Brown Argus	Rock-rose, stork's-bill
Brown Hairstreak	Blackthorn
Camberwell Beauty	Willow and sallow
Chalk Hill Blue	Horse-shoe vetch
Chequered Skipper	Slender false brome grass
Clouded Yellow	Lucerne and various clovers
Comma	Elm, nettle, hop, gooseberry, currant
Common Blue	Bird's-foot trefoil, black medick, rest harrow
Dark Green Fritillary	Dog-violet and cultivated violas
Dingy Skipper	Bird's-foot trefoil
Duke of Burgundy Fritillary	Primrose, cowslip
Essex Skipper	Couch-grass
Gatekeeper	Almost any lush grass
Glanville Fritillary	Narrow-leaved plantain
Grayling	Various downland grasses
Green Hairstreak	Flower buds of dogwood, broom, furze, on bilberry further north, and on boggy ground
Green-veined White	Charlock, hedge mustard, horse-radish, cuckoo flower, watercress
Grizzled Skipper	Wild strawberry, silverweed, cinquefoil, agrimony
Heath Fritillary	Cow wheat
High Brown Fritillary	Dog-violet
	Flower heads. *Spring:* holly, dogwood, buckthorn. *Autumn:* ivy
Large Blue	Wild thyme blossoms
Large Copper	Great water dock
Large Heath	Beaked rush; grasses in captivity (*Poa annua*)

STUDYING INSECTS

Large Skipper	Slender false brome grass
Large Tortoiseshell	Elm, sallow. Oviposits in rings on twigs
Large White	Cabbage family, horse-radish, garden nasturtium
Long-tailed Blue	Everlasting pea
Lulworth Skipper	Most grasses
Marbled White	Most downland grasses. Scatters eggs loose
Marsh Fritillary	Devil's-bit scabious; in captivity: snowberry, honeysuckle
Mazarine Blue	Clovers
Meadow Brown	Most grasses
Milkweed	Various milkweeds
New Clouded Yellow	Horse-shoe vetch
Orange Tip	Hedge mustard, cuckoo flower, sweet rocket
Painted Lady	Thistles, burdock
Pale Clouded Yellow	Bird's-foot trefoil, lucerne
Peacock	Stinging-nettle
Pearl-bordered Fritillary	Dog-violet. Will oviposit on dead bracken in captivity
Purple Emperor	Sallow
Purple Hairstreak	Oak
Queen of Spain Fritillary	Dog-violet, heart's-ease
Red Admiral	Stinging-nettle
Ringlet	Various grasses
Scotch Argus	Blue moor grass
Short-tailed Blue	Bird's-foot trefoil
Silver-spotted Skipper	Sheep's fescue grass
Silver-studded Blue	Blossoms of heath and heather, furze, broom, etc.
Silver-washed Fritillary	Dog-violet, cultivated violas. Will lay amongst old curtain netting pinned on sides of cage
Small Blue.	Kidney vetch blossoms
Small Copper	Sheep's sorrel
Small Heath	Most grasses
Small Mountain Ringlet	Mat grass
Small Pearl-bordered Fritillary	Dog-violet. Will lay amongst dried bracken in captivity
Small Skipper	Cat's-tail grass, soft creeping grass

FOOD PLANTS OF BRITISH BUTTERFLIES

Small Tortoiseshell	Stinging-nettle
Small White	Cabbage family, hedge mustard, horse-radish
Speckled Wood	Various grasses, including woodland species
Swallow-tail	Hog's fennel, wild angelica, carrot, fennel
Wall	Various grasses
White Admiral	Honeysuckle; snowberry in captivity
White Letter Hairstreak	Wych elm, common elm
Wood White	Tuberous pea

APPENDIX IV

Books, Magazines, Societies and Supplies

A large number of books are published on insects, mostly on butterflies but quite a number on moths. When choosing a book, make quite sure what it is you require from it. If you want it for naming specimens, make sure it covers all or the great majority of the group in which you are interested and is not of a very general nature with just a selection of plates of the more prominent species.

There are magazines on entomology such as *The Entomologist*, (41 Queen's Gate, London, S.W.7), *The Entomologist's Monthly Magazine*, (Dr. B. M. Hobby, 7 Thorncliffe Road, Oxford, OX2 7BA) and the *Entomologist's Gazette*, (353 Hanworth Road, Hampton, Middlesex). The first two mentioned are monthly and are on general entomology with the second having a strong bias towards Coleoptera. The *Gazette* is quarterly and confines itself to the British Isles. These magazines publish interesting records, but the majority of the papers are of a specialized and technical nature.

The largest entomological society is the Royal Entomological Society of London, whose offices and meeting rooms are at 41 Queen's Gate, London, S.W.7. The society has the finest library on entomology in the world and publishes a great deal of material on the subject but of a highly technical nature. It also publishes the handbooks already mentioned and these are the best textbooks for the advanced student.

The British Entomological and Natural History Society draws its membership from all over the British Isles and holds fortnightly meetings, as well as a series of field meetings and an annual exhibition at the British Museum (Natural History) to which collectors come from all parts. This

STUDYING INSECTS

society publishes its *Proceedings and Transactions* in one volume each year, and these contain many interesting papers and reports of interest to the amateur as well as to the more advanced collector. The society also houses a very fine and comprehensive insect collection and library at its rooms in The Alpine Club, 74 South Audley Street, London, W.1. This collection is available on meeting nights and is most useful for comparing captures, and willing help is given to the young or inexperienced collector by other members at both indoor and outdoor meetings.

The British Trust for Entomology caters for advanced entomologists and publishes *Transactions of the Society for British Entomology* (c/o 41 Queen's Gate, London, S.W.7).

The Amateur Entomologists' Society is primarily for younger, less advanced students of insect life and publishes a wide range of leaflets on many groups as well as a regular *Bulletin*. A Geographical Index of members helps to bring fellow students in an area into touch with each other. The address is R. D. Hilliard, Hon. Advertising Secretary, 18 Golf Close, Stanmore, Middlesex.

Catalogues of new books and equipment may be obtained from Messrs Watkins & Doncaster, Four Throws, Hawkhurst, Kent. Chemicals, stains and reagents for microscopic work may be obtained from Messrs Gerrard & Haig Ltd, Worthing Road, East Preston, Sussex. Second-hand books and scientific papers on entomology are obtainable from E. W. Classey at 353 Hanworth Road, Hampton, Middlesex, and livestock, particularly foreign butterflies and silk moths, from World Wide Butterflies Ltd, Over Compton, Sherborne, Dorset.

BOOKS RECOMMENDED

Books marked with an asterisk are out of print but may be consulted in most large public libraries.

T. G. Howarth, *South's British Butterflies*
W. J. Stokoe, *The Observer's Book of Butterflies*
R. L. E. Ford, *The Observer's Book of the Larger Moths*

Wayside and Woodland Series
R. South, *The Moths of the British Isles* (2 vols)
W. J. Stokoe and G. H. T. Stovin, *The Caterpillars of the British Butterflies;* and *The Caterpillars of British Moths* (2 vols)*
B. P. Beirne, *British Pyralid and Plume Moths*
C. N. Colyer and C. O. Hammond, *Flies of the British Isles* (Diptera)
T. R. E. Southwood and D. Leston, *Land and Water Bugs of the British Isles*
E. F. Linssen, *Beetles of the British Isles* (2 vols)

BOOKS, MAGAZINES, SOCIETIES, SUPPLIES

Cynthia Longfield, *The Dragonflies of the British Isles**
E. Step, *Bees, Wasps, Ants, and Allied Insects of the British Isles**

All the above contain extensive coloured plates of species and are published by Messrs Frederick Warne & Co. Ltd as is F. A. Urquhart's *Introducing the Insect*, which is a useful beginner's guide to the recognition, life-histories and habits of the main group of insects.

H. Oldroyd, *Insects and their World*, published by the British Museum (Natural History), is another good introduction to insects and how they live and behave.

A. D. Imms, *A General Textbook of Entomology* (9th ed.), published by Methuen & Co. A standard work on insects.

V. B. Wigglesworth, *Insect physiology*, published by Methuen & Co.

L. T. Ford, *A Guide to the Smaller British Lepidoptera*, published by the South London Society. This has no plates but gives the life-histories of some 1,370 moths with indices of the foods and food plants and of the insects with cross-references, so that if you are breeding microlepidoptera it is a great aid to identification.

The Royal Entomological Society publishes a series of handbooks for the identification of British insects.

GENERAL INDEX

Numbers in italics indicate pages on which line drawings appear

Aeschna, 44
Ammonia, 43
Anaesthetic, 38
Ants, collecting, 100
, food for, 112
, keeping, 109
, wood, 112
Assembling moths, 33
Attracting insects, 124

Bait, 41
Beating, 63, Plate 10
 tray, 36, Plates 2, 11
Beechwood creosote, 108
Bees, humble, 118
, mason, 118
, plasterer, 118
Beetle, burying, 41, 42, Plate 5
, cockchafer, Plate 9
, dor, Plate 8
, glow-worm, 23
, museum, 54, 95, 107
, rose chafer, 42, Plate 8
, Rove, 42
, stag, *20*, 21
, larvae of, 120
Beetles, 12, 16, 18, 40–42, 50, 55, 80
Beetle trap, 40–42, *42*
Blow-fly, 128, 129
Book pattern boxes, 95
Boxes, collecting, 33, 38–39
, store, 94–96, *95*
Breeding, 60–85
 cages, 68–69, *68, 70*
Buddleia, 32, 60
Buddleia alternifolia, 125
 globosa, 125
Bug, Bed, 132
Bugs, 16, 17
Bupleurum fruticosum, 40
Butterflies, attracting, 124–127

Cabinets, 96, *98*
, converting, 99, *100*
, reconditioning, 101

Caddis-fly, 15, 18, Plate 5
Cages, 68–69, *68, 70*
Camera lucida, *122*
Camphor cell, 96, 99, 107
Carbolic acid, 75, 108
Carbon tetrachloride, 43, 44, 104, 130
Card points, 56, *57*
Caterpillars, care of young, 72
, rearing of, 68
Chalcids, 56
Chrysalis, *see* Pupa
Chrysalis stage, 75
Cicadas, 16, 17, Plate 4
 grubs of, Plates 1, 4
Cockroach, 15, 17, 23, 129, 131
Coleophora, 83
Coleoptera, 12, 39. *See also* Beetles
Collecting ants, 110
 from flowers, 39
 larvae, 63
 on holiday, 45
Cork, composition, 100
 linoleum, 96
, virgin, 96
Corking drawers, 100
Cricket, Bush, Plates 13, 16
, Mole, 22
, Wood, Plate 16
Cyanide, 43

Data labels, 49, 92, 93–94
Degreasing, 104–105
Depressaria, 36
Diptera, 13, 18, 22, 38, 39, 40, 55, 128
Disease causes, 69
Dragonflies, 14–15, 17, 21, 22, 23, 28, 40, 44, 55, 106–107
Drawers, slatted, 97
Drying insects, 53

Earwigs, 15, *56*
Egg laying, 35, 60
Emeralds, 44, 45
Emergence, 77

GENERAL INDEX

Envelopes, storage, 45–46
Ethyl acetate, 38, 43, 44, 45, 104

Feeding butterflies, 61
Flower-pots, 80, 83
, grinding, 80–81
Fluoron, 113
Forceps, entomological, 51
Forcing pupae, 79
Formicarium, 109–113
Freeze-drying, 44, 91
Fruit-fly, 128, 129

Gelechia, 36
Glass cells, *108*
Glass-topped boxes, 33
Grasshopper, Large Marsh, Plate 13
Grasshoppers, setting, 55
Grease, 103
Gum tragacanth, 56

Hawk moths, 21, 62, 67, 71, 77, 78
Hemiptera, 15–16, 17, 39
Hibernating butterflies, 125, 126
Hogweed, 42
Homoptera, 17, 39
Honeycomb moth, 129, 130
Honey-dew, 33
House-fly, 128, 129
Humble-bees, 56, 117–118
Hybrids, 77
Hymenoptera, 13–14, 18, 38, 39, 40, 56, 114, 133, 134
Hypodermic syringe, 44–45

Identification, insect, 133–135
Illustrating insects, 121–123
Insect cultures, 128–132
  deterrents, 107

Killing, 42
  bottle, 39, 43
Kite net, 24, *25*, 37, Plates 2, 3

Labelling, 93–94
Lamps, incandescent, 31–32, *31*
, mercury vapour, 29, 30

Larvae blowing, 86–89
, colouring, 90
, preserving, 86–92
, sleeving, 69, Plate 10
Laurel leaves, 44
Lill pins, 50, 52, 56
Locusts, 15, 17, 21
, migratory, 129, 131–132
Lucerne, 62

Mating moths, 34
Meal moth, 129, 130
Mealworm, 129, 130
Meconium, 131
Mercury vapour traps, 29, 124, Plate 7
Microgasterinae, 56
Microlepidoptera, collecting, 67
Mites, 54, 55, 95, 107, Plate 8
Moths, assembling, 33
Mould, 75, 108
Mounting insects, 55
  larvae, 89–90, *90*
Museum beetle, 54, 95, 107
Muslin, 71

Naphthalene balls, 107–108
Naphthalene, excess of, 107–108
, flaked, 46, 55, 107
Needle, setting, *53*
Net bags, 26
  forceps, 39, *40*
Nets, 24–25
Nettle, 60, 64, 127
Noctuid larvae, 65

Observation nests, 118
Oxalic acid, 45

Pampel's mixture, 92
Paper cutting, 102
, drawer lining, 102
  envelopes, 45, *46*
, removing, 101
Paradichlorbenzene, 55, 107
Parasite rearing, 81
Paste, for papering, 102
Peat linings, 97
Pin corrosion, 102, 103–104
Pinning specimens, *51*

147

GENERAL INDEX

Pinning stages, 57, 58–59, *58*
Pins, entomological, 49, 50, 103
Photography, 121, 123, Plate 15
Plant tubs, 83–85, *84*
Plastic foam, 97
Plume moths, 80, 83
Polyporous pith, *49*, 107
Pooter, *37*, 38
Preservation chemicals, 55
Preserving solutions, 91–92
Pupa digging, 78, Plate 11
  forcing, 79
  storage, 76–77
Pupation, methods of, 75–76
Pyrales, 80

Red Ant, 110
Refrigerator, 73, 74, 75, 126
Relaxing, 45
  tin, 45–47, *47*
Repairs, 105–107
Repapering, 99, 102
Rubber solution, 105

Saw-flies, 13, 18, 23, 80
  , larvae of, 65, *66*
Scissors net, *see* Net forceps
Senecio clivorum, 126
  desdemona, 126
Setting, 47, *48*, *51*, *52*, *54*
  board, 48, 49, 53
  case, Plate 6
  needle, *53*
Sex, of pupae, 77, 78
Silk-worms, 73–74

Sleeving, 71
Sleeving materials, 71
Smoking insects, 35–36, Plate 2
Spiders, attracting, 125
Staging small insects, 49
Storage, 46, 94
Sub-terrarium, *119*
Sugaring, 32–33, Plate 6
Sweeping, 37, 39, 67

Tineids, 80
Titanium dioxide, 101
Toluene, 104
Traps, assembling, 34
  , beetle, 40–41, *42*
  , flight, 40, *41*
  , insect, 40
  , M.V., 29, Plate 7
  , wasp, 114–115

Verdigris, 103

Wasp, Tree, Plate 16
  , Wood, 21, Plate 9
Wasps, 13, 18, 19, 114–116
  , tracking, 116
'White' caterpillars, 64
  pupae, 76
Whitening chemicals, 101
Wing patching, 75, 106
Winter collecting, 82
Wood's glass envelope, 30

Zinc oxide, 101

INDEX TO LEPIDOPTERA

Butterflies – Rhopalocera

Adonis Blue, *Lysandra bellargus* Rott., 108
Brimstone, *Gonepteryx rhamni* Linn., 3, 4, 27
Brown Hairstreak, *Thecla betulae* Linn., 63
Chalk Hill Blue, *Lysandra coridon coridon* Pod., 7, 27
Clouded Yellow, *Colias croceus* Fourc., 43, 61
Comma, *Polygonia c-album* Linn., 61, 125
Gatekeeper, *Pyronia tithonus* Linn., 65
Glanville Fritillary, *Melitaea cinxia* Linn., 5
Grayling, *Hipparchia semele* Linn., 65
Holly Blue, *Celastrina argiolus* Linn., 66, 124
Large Blue, *Maculinea arion* Linn., 2, 3
Large Copper, *Lycaena dispar* Haworth, 1
Large Tortoiseshell, *Nymphalis polychloros* Linn., 61, 125
Large White, *Pieris brassicae* Linn., 87
Marbled White, *Melanargia galathea* Linn., 7, 65
Marsh Fritillary, *Euphydryas aurinia* Rott., 5, 85
Meadow Brown, *Maniola jurtina* Linn., 65
Orange-tip, *Anthocharis cardamines* Linn., 3, 4, 60
Painted Lady, *Vanessa cardui* Linn., 42
Peacock, *Inachis io* Linn., 64, 125
Purple Emperor, *Apatura iris* Linn., 7–8, 27, 49, 65
Purple Hairstreak, *Quercusia quercus* Linn., 63
Red Admiral, *Vanessa atalanta* Linn., 27, 42, 64, 103, 125, 126
Silver-washed Fritillary, *Argynnis paphia* Linn., 60
Skippers, Hesperiidae, 65
Small Copper, *Lycaena phlaeas* Linn., 27, 65
Small Tortoiseshell, *Aglais urticae* Linn., 64, 125
Speckled Wood, *Pararge aegeria* Linn., 7, 65
Wall, *Lasiommata megera* Linn., 65
White Admiral, *Ladoga camilla* Linn., 6, 60, 65
White Letter Hairstreak, *Strymonidia w-album* Knoch, 63

Moths – Heterocera

Beautiful Yellow Underwing, *Anarta myrtilli* Linn., 30, 67
Blair's Wainscot, *Sedina büttneri* Her., 10
Browntail, *Euproctis chrysorrhoea* Linn., 72
Burnet moths, Zygaenidae, 11, 89
Cinnabar, *Callimorpha jacobaeae* Linn., 29, Plate 12
Convolvulus Hawk, *Agrius convolvuli* Linn., 27, 127
Cudweed Shark, *Cucullia gnaphalii* Hübn., 67
Death's Head Hawk, *Acherontia atropos* Linn., 79
Emperor Moth, *Saturnia pavonia* Linn., 34
Eyed Hawk, *Smerinthus ocellata* Linn., 77, 78, 103
Fox Moth, *Macrothylacia rubi* Linn., 29, 72, 75
Garden Tiger, *Arctia caja* Linn., 87, 129, 130

INDEX TO LEPIDOPTERA

Goat Moth, *Cossus cossus* Linn., 76
Isle of Wight Wave, *Sterrha humiliata* Hufn., 8
Lackey Moth, *Malacosoma neustria* Linn., 63
Lappet Moth, *Gastropacha quercifolia* Linn., 67
Large Elephant Hawk, *Deilephila elpenor* Linn., 62, 72, 75, 77
Light Orange Underwing, *Archiearis notha* Hübn., 9, 36
Lime Hawk, *Mimas tiliae* Linn., 62, 71
Mother of Pearl, *Pleuroptya ruralis* Scop., 64
Oak Eggar, *Lasiocampa quercus* Linn., 33, 72
Pine Hawk, *Hyloicus pinastri* Linn., 105
Plume moths, Pterophoridae, 80, 83
Poplar Hawk, *Laothoe populi* Linn., 62, 77, 78
Privet Hawk, *Sphinx ligustri* Linn., 62, 75
Puss Moth, *Cerura vinula* Linn., 62, 103
Red Underwing, *Catocala nupta* Linn., 35

Nomenclature: Kloet and Hincks Check List, Revised 1972